The Adventure of
NATURE PHOTOGRAPHY

The Adventure of NATURE PHOTOGRAPHY

Tim Fitzharris

Hurtig Publishers Ltd.
Edmonton

To Sheryl

Hurtig Publishers Ltd.
10560 – 105 Street
Edmonton, Alberta
Canada T5H 2W7

Canadian Cataloguing in Publication Data

Fitzharris, Tim, 1948–
    The adventure of nature photography

Bibliography: p.
ISBN 0-88830-250-9 (bound).—ISBN 0-88830-237-1 (pbk.)

1. Nature photography.   I. Title.
TR721.F57   778.9′3   C83-091232-0

Printed and bound in Canada

Contents

Acknowledgements

I would like to thank my wife, Sheryl, who stitched blinds, typed correspondence and manuscripts, criticized my pictures and encouraged my photographic endeavours over a number of years. Since I began taking pictures, my son, Jim, has been my chief helper, and frequent companion on field excursions.

Special arrangements for the use of photographic equipment supplied by Canon Canada Ltd. were made by Bayne Stanley. John Doremus provided assistance in making the picture of the ferruginous hawk; Mark Fitzharris helped me take the picture of the turtle.

Some of the information in the text has appeared previously in modified form in articles that I wrote for *Photo Life*, *Petersen's Photographic* and *Nature Canada*.

The support of all the editors, especially Les Line and Arnet Sheppard, who have chosen my pictures for their publications is greatly appreciated.

I want to thank my subjects, particularly the birds and mammals, just for being there.

Introduction

Nature photography is many things to many people. It is considered by some as art, by others as "hunting" with film rather than bullets. It can be a relaxing hobby or an all-consuming passion. It may be recreation to be enjoyed while canoeing or backpacking or the primary motive that takes one into the wilderness. There is no season, schedule nor time of day that excludes it. Nature photography's subject matter is as much the twinkle in a dewdrop as it is the courting rites of a sandhill crane or the eruption of an Hawaiian volcano. It can be practised readily in the backyard, in Banff National Park, or New York's Central Park. Whatever your present occupation, be it electrician, teacher, doctor, or civil servant, you can find a time and place to experience the pleasures of nature photography.

The environmental movements of the late 1960s generated a revitalized appreciation for the practical, as well as spiritual, values, that nature holds. Wildlife is no longer a prey to be captured, but rather something that captures us—with its beauty, honesty and fragility. Nature has always been a source of inspiration for scientists, philosophers and artists. Society needs such explorers to bring their understandings and expressions of truth and reality to the workaday world. The ecological and artistic insights that you achieve as a nature photographer will attain only a small measure of their value unless shared with others.

I hope this book will help you to look at nature in a clear and perceptive way, and that the photographs you make will, in turn, help others do the same.

Suggested Reading

Allen, A.A., *Stalking Birds with Color Camera*. National Geographic Society, Washington, D.C., 1951 (re field experience)

Angel, Heather, *Nature Photography, Its Art and Technique*. Fountain Press, King's Langley, England, 1972

Blaker, A.A., *Field Photography—Beginning and Advanced Techniques*. W.H. Freeman & Co., San Francisco, 1979

Dalton, Stephen, *Borne on the Wind*. Reader's Digest Press, New York, 1975 (re insects)

Ettlinger, D.M. Turner, *Natural History Photography*. Academic Press, New York, 1975

Hosking, Eric, *Wildlife Photography*. Praeger, New York, 1973

Izzi, Guglielmo and Mezzatesta, Francesco, *The Complete Manual of Nature Photography*. Harper & Row, New York, 1981

Kinne, Russ, *The Complete Book of Nature Photography*. Amphoto, New York, 1971

LIFE Library of Photography, *Photographing Nature*. (Revised edition.) Time-Life Books Inc., Alexandria, Virginia, 1981

McElroy, Jr., T.P., *The New Handbook of Attracting Birds*. Alfred A. Knopf, New York, 1961

Owens, William J., *Close-up Photography*. Peterson Publishing Co., Los Angeles, 1975

Oxford Scientific Films, *Focus on Nature*. Faber and Faber Ltd., London, 1981

Patterson, Freeman, *Photography & the Art of Seeing*. Van Nostrand Reinhold Ltd., Toronto, 1979

Patterson, Freeman, *Photography for the Joy of It*. Van Nostrand Reinhold Ltd., Toronto, 1977

Porter, Eliot, *Birds of North America*. E.P. Dutton & Co., New York, 1972 (re field experience)

Stokes, D.W., *A Guide to the Behavior of Common Birds*. Little Brown and Co., Boston, 1979

Warham, John, *The Technique of Photographing Birds*. The Focal Press, London, 1956

Wilson, Arnold, *Creative Techniques in Nature Photography*. J.B. Lippincott Co., Philadelphia, 1979

The Mechanics of Nature Photography

CHAPTER ONE

The Nature Photographer's Camera

The camera is a machine that is used to make recordings of reflected light. In simple terms, it is a box with a lens attached to one end. This lens gathers up light and directs it onto a piece of photographic film positioned at the opposite end.

The operation of a camera is easy. It generally involves controlling the amount of light that enters the box, and focusing this light precisely on the film. Almost all of the knobs, buttons, scales, dials, cranks, switches, and levers that adorn the shapely bodies of modern cameras are used to accomplish these two operations.

Basic Camera Types

A camera is classified according to its viewing system, which is the means by which the photographer is able to see just what he is photographing. More specific classification is based on the size of the film used by the camera, referred to as the "camera format."

The Viewfinder Camera

With this type of camera the photographer looks through a small window (the viewfinder) which is separate from the lens that directs the light onto the film. Because the photographer, in effect, sees the scene from a slightly different angle than does the film, framing inaccuracy, called "parallax error," is apparent, especially at close range. As a result, these cameras are unsuitable for photographing wildflowers, insects, small birds or anything else requiring a close-up approach. The viewing system also makes lens interchange impractical, and this feature is provided in a limited way on only a few, very expensive models. This type of camera includes instamatic and rangefinder cameras of various formats. (Fig. 1A)

The Viewfinder Camera
Parallax Error

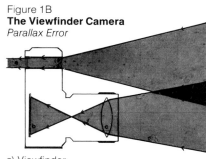

a) Viewfinder
b) Film
c) Lens

Figure 1A
The View Camera
Heavy and Unwieldy

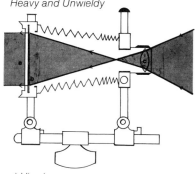

a) Viewing screen
    (ground glass)
b) Film
c) Lens

Figure 1C
The Single Lens Reflex
An Ideal Design

a) Viewfinder   d) Mirror
b) Pentaprism   e) Lens
c) Film

The View Camera

The lens of the view camera transmits light directly from the subject onto a semi-transparent, glass view screen called the "ground glass". This provides the photographer with a dim but exact image of what is to be recorded on film. For better viewing, the photographer shrouds himself and the rear of the camera with a black cloth. Once the image has been precisely focused and the exposure controls adjusted, the ground-glass screen is simply replaced by a sheet of film and the picture is taken.

The camera body itself incorporates a leather bellows between the lens and film holder, which permits the photographer to tilt and shift these parts independently. This allows increased control over focusing and per-spective problems. Normally used for landscape and still-life photography when finely detailed images are required, the view camera is generally not suitable for nature subjects. Although the image is accurate, it is seen upside down and reversed by the photographer. This makes photographing a moving animal very difficult. Also, the film is changed manually, one sheet at a time, making rapid shooting impossible. Furthermore, the view camera is too large and heavy for convenient field use. (Fig. 1B)

The Single-lens Reflex Camera

This camera design also permits the photographer to view the subject through the lens that directs the image onto the film, thus assuring fram-ing and focusing accuracy in all circumstances. This is accomplished by a mirror, inside the camera, which reflects the image upward through a kind of periscope (called a "pentaprism") to the viewfinder. The photographer sees the scene right side up and unreversed. The mirror is hinged and swings out of the way just prior to exposure, permitting the light to reach the film. The major advantage of this viewing system is that it works equally well with any lens the photographer cares to mount on the cam-era. Single-lens reflex cameras in a variety of formats are available, but by far the most popular type uses 35-mm film. (Fig. 1C)

The Ideal Camera for Nature Photography

The most suitable camera for nature photography is the type that many amateurs own—the 35-mm, single-lens reflex. Some of the reasons are the following:

- The camera is compact and lightweight, and thus easily portable in the field.
- It operates quickly and conveniently, making it suitable for active subjects.**(1)***
- The camera itself is the nucleus of an extensive system of inter-

*Numbers in bold type refer to the photographs.

11

changeable lenses, motor drives and close-up accessories, that permits photography of virtually any subject of natural history.

- The film is relatively inexpensive. This makes the overshooting (taking many exposures) of unpredictable action (*e.g.*, a bird in flight) economically feasible, in addition to everyday use.
- In the hands of a skilled photographer, it will produce pictures of the highest professional quality.

Operating a 35-mm Single-lens Reflex Camera

The camera's operating manual usually provides a comprehensive explanation of the machine's various functions. At first, this information may appear rather intimidating, but it is easily grasped after the photographer masters a few of the basic operations. My present camera has forty-one different operating devices incorporated in its design, but I only use seven of them when taking pictures. They are the following:

- THE SHUTTER RELEASE BUTTON is pushed to take the picture.
- THE FILM-WINDING LEVER is used to move the exposed film aside and bring a fresh section into position.
- THE FOCUSING RING is used to focus the image precisely on the film.
- THE APERTURE RING controls the diaphragm, a device which changes the size of the aperture in order to regulate the amount of light reaching the film.
- THE SHUTTER SPEED DIAL is also used to regulate exposure. It controls the amount of time the shutter remains open.
- THE LIGHT METER SWITCH turns on the light meter, a gauge which helps the photographer decide on the shutter speed and aperture size to be used for the exposure.
- THE DEPTH-OF-FIELD PREVIEW LEVER is an aid to composition which allows the photographer to view the relative sharpness of various parts of the scene before exposure. (Fig. 2)

The only other controls of major significance are associated with loading and unloading film.

Taking a Picture: Routine Procedure

It is helpful for the beginner to conduct the various operations of picture-taking in a routine manner. The steps that follow are particularly suited for nature photography, where depth of field (controlled by the aperture setting) is usually an artistic priority.

Step 1. Turn on the light meter.
Step 2. Frame the scene.
Step 3. Focus on the most important part.

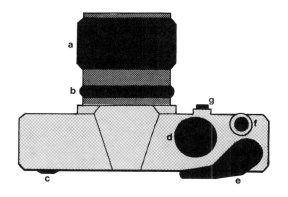

Figure 2
Basic Controls of the 55 mm SLR

a) Focusing ring
b) Aperture ring
c) Light meter switch
d) Shutter speed dial
e) Film wind lever
f) Shutter release button
g) Depth of field preview lever

Step 4. Set the aperture ring.
Step 5. View the depth of field.
Step 6. Set the shutter speed for the desired exposure.
Step 7. Push the shutter release button.
Step 8. Wind the film.

Buying a 35-mm Single-lens Reflex Camera

A person with little photographic experience is likely to be confused by
the wide variety of brands and models of 35-mm, single-lens reflex cameras on the market. Unfortunately, it is difficult to find a camera salesper-
son with sufficient expertise to provide accurate information or valid
advice. However, the beginner, assuming he intends to give photography a
full and serious trial, has nothing to worry about provided he follows these
suggestions:

- Buy a camera that has manual exposure control. Exposure determination is more accurate and convenient in the majority of situations
  if the photographer controls it himself. Such a camera is also less
  expensive and more durable than automatic models.
- If you do purchase an automatic exposure model, be sure it is of
  the aperture priority type, and that it has optional, convenient-to-
  operate manual exposure control.
- Buy a camera that has a depth-of-field preview lever. Complete
  control of composition is impossible without this feature.
- Don't be afraid to buy a used camera in good condition rather than a
  new one. If the camera appears to be well taken care of, and the controls function properly, it will probably provide many more years of
  trouble-free service. Choose a brand with an established reputation
  such as Canon, Minolta, Nikon, Olympus, or Pentax. Buy film with
  the money that is saved.

A camera which satisfies these conditions will be a simple, easy-to-operate instrument of professional calibre.

Binoculars

No matter what type of nature activity you become involved in, a pair of binoculars is essential. They help in two ways. They will enable you to interpret or read conditions that might otherwise call for a close approach: for example, identifying a plant species or determining whether a nest is occupied or abandoned. They will also allow you to study animals that flee from the close presence of humans.

Binocular sizes are described by two numbers. The first tells how much the subject will be magnified. The second gives an indication of how much light is passing through the lens by denoting the diameter of the front or objective lens element in millimetres. A pair of 7 x 35 binoculars would magnify, or bring one closer to, the subject by a factor of seven and be quite bright enough for daytime use. Their light weight and compactness make them the best choice for wildlife watching. A pair of 7 x 50 binoculars has the same magnifying power but allows more light to pass through, giving a brighter image between sun-down and sun-up. Binoculars with more magnifying power will provide a closer look at the subject. However, they also have a narrower angle of view, and usually it is difficult enough to locate a fleeing animal in the viewing field of seven-power binoculars.

Don't Leave Home Without It

It is almost as important to place a tripod beneath a camera as it is to put film inside it. I use a tripod for almost every type of shooting and credit the use of this humble apparatus with a good deal of my success in and enjoyment of nature photography.

It is difficult to be sure that one is achieving the maximum sharpness or resolution of which a lens or film is capable unless the camera is held rock-steady during exposure. Without the aid of some inanimate device like a tripod, camera steadiness is unlikely, resulting in considerable deterioration of technical quality.

A tripod is especially valuable when one is using telephoto lenses or doing most types of close-up work in natural light. Without it, night photography is impossible, as is shooting colour film in the dim, dramatic light of dawn or dusk. Even when photographing at midday with colour film, one cannot take advantage of the camera's full range of f stops and shutter speeds without using a tripod—unless, of course, one is content with fuzzy images.

Composition and the application of creative approaches to image-making both benefit from the use of a tripod. Physically freed from his machine the photographer can achieve an unhurried, thorough analysis of the image without experiencing mounting impatience due to cramped arms and hands, or an awkward body stance. Due to the stability of the camera, the scene, as presented through the viewfinder, readily takes on the inanimate, two-dimensional quality of a finished photograph. Thus the photographer can more accurately anticipate the effectiveness of the composition. Although the tripod may at first seem like an impediment to the creative process—another distracting mechanism with which the photographer must contend—in practice it has the opposite effect. It allows more convenient control of technical operations such as exposure adjustment, shutter release, focusing and setting depth of field. Also, such stream-lining of routine procedures allows the photographer to apply more attention and energy to the artistic aspects of picture-making.

A Sturdy Set of Legs

There are a number of special factors to consider when choosing a tripod for nature photography:

- Avoid tripods with leg locks of the twisting collar-ring type. These mechanisms easily become clogged with dirt and grit, making extension of the legs difficult or impossible. Lever or clip-lock legs are preferable for outside work.
- Avoid tripods with leg braces attached to the centre column. This feature adds little practical stability and means that the legs must always be spread apart an equal distance—a decided handicap when one is trying to set up the tripod on uneven or rocky terrain.
- Choose a tripod that permits removal and reinsertion of the centre column so that the tripod head hangs between the legs. This is an indispensable feature for working with ground-hugging subjects like wildflowers.
- A panning ball-and-socket head is preferable to most types of pan/tilt heads. The camera can be positioned more freely and can easily be operated with only a single control. There are no awkward levers to spear one's throat or get caught in the legs if one is working at a low level with the centre column inverted.
- Buy a tripod that is high enough. The tripod head should be at eye-level when the legs (but not the centre column) are extended.
- Keep in mind that the best manufacturers sell the tripod head and legs separately. This makes it easier to assemble a combination that is suitable for nature photography.
- Don't skimp on quality. Count on paying at least as much for a tripod as for an extra lens.

Pneumatic Shutter Release

Even when the photographer is using a tripod, it is almost impossible to trip the shutter by hand without jarring the camera. To preserve stability, a pneumatic (or bulb) shutter release should be used. Operating on air pressure forced through a thin, flexible tube, this inexpensive device is less likely to transmit hand vibrations to the camera than is the more conventional cable release. It can also be activated by the mouth, leaving both hands free to adjust camera and tripod controls, an especially valuable feature in photographing active subjects. When remote camera operation is needed, (photography at bird nests for example) most pneumatic releases can easily be extended to lengths of ten metres or more by attaching additional tubing.

A cable release is necessary for shooting in dim light or other situations when the shutter must be kept open manually for long periods of time (usually for exposures exceeding one second unless the camera has an extended shutter speed range).

The Well-Dressed Photographer

The major advantage of the 35-mm, single-lens reflex camera is its adaptability to a wide range of accessories. The larger systems offer more than 140 different attachments for a single camera model. Needless to say, you don't need them all, nor will I attempt to provide a list of the equipment that the well-dressed nature photographer is likely to have. It is a common, but mistaken, assumption that there is a direct correlation between a photographer's abilities, and the extent and quality of his equipment. Generally, the more attention the photographer pays to hardware the less attention he pays to photography.

The most sensible way to decide what accessories are needed is to take lots of pictures. Don't consider buying anything until a recurring need develops from actual experience in the field. In this way the photographer will acquire a stream-lined system, naturally tailored to his personal approach and interests, and avoid unnecessary equipment expenditures.

CHAPTER TWO

Lenses for Far and Wide

When light strikes an object, it reflects from the surface in all directions. The lens is designed to collect and form these light rays into a coherent image on film in the same way the lens of the eye directs light onto the retina. Without a lens the object would be recorded on film as an unintelligible blur.

Lens Size

Lenses are classified according to focal length and aperture size. The focal length is expressed in millimetres and measures the distance from the optical centre of the lens to the film. Focal-length numbers are important because they tell how much the subject will be magnified on film. For example, a 100-mm lens will magnify the subject twice as much as a 50-mm lens and four times as much as a 25-mm lens, provided all pictures are taken at the same distance.

The diameter of the lens opening is important because it determines how much light the lens can deliver to the film during any single exposure. It is measured relative to the lens focal length and is expressed by f stop numbers. A lens with an aperture size of f2 has an opening with a diameter half of its focal length. This measuring system produces the peculiar result that large f stop numbers designate small apertures and vice versa. However, because the f stop number actually expresses a ratio, it means that f5.6 on a 50-mm lens will let in the same amount of light as f5.6 on a 600-mm lens. Thus the f stop number represents a constant value which makes exposure calculations rather simple once one becomes familiar with the system.

Types of Lenses

The most important characteristic of a lens is its focal length, and lenses are typically referred to as being either normal, telephoto or wide-angle.

- The NORMAL LENS takes in approximately the same angle of view as, and hence produces a degree of magnification similar to, that of the human eye. The focal length of the normal lens is equal to the diagonal measurement of a section of the film the camera uses. Thus, for a 35-mm camera, the normal lens has a focal length of about 50 mm. A camera that uses larger film will have a normal lens with a relatively longer focal length.
- The TELEPHOTO LENS works like a telescope to magnify the subject. It has a focal length longer than 50 mm with some "super" telephotos ranging to 2000 mm. The telephoto lens is one of the most useful tools for the nature photographer.
- The WIDE-ANGLE LENS takes in a wider angle of view than the normal lens and has a focal length less than 50 mm. Its most obvious effect is to reduce the size of the subject and increase the apparent camera-to-subject distance.

Special Lenses

- A ZOOM LENS provides a continuous range of focal lengths in one package. Present lenses have roughly a two-to-one zooming ratio. For example, a wide-angle zoom might provide all focal lengths from 25 mm to 50 mm and a telephoto zoom might range from 100 mm to 200 mm. There are a number of advantages to the zoom lens. It permits the most minute adjustments in framing, making it convenient for landscape photography or other situations when there may be some difficulty in adjusting the camera position, such as working in a blind, or on a narrow cliff. The zoom lens can often do the job of several fixed-focal-length lenses, and it is less expensive and easier to carry.
- A MACRO LENS is able to focus at much closer range than standard lenses. At the same time it is also quite suitable for regular distance work, making it ideal for the nature photographer who may be shooting a butterfly close-up one instant and a passing deer the next. The person seriously interested in natural history photography should consider purchasing a camera equipped with a macro lens of normal focal length rather than the standard lens that is usually sold with the camera.
- A MIRROR LENS is a special type of telephoto lens which uses mirrors in the optical design to decrease the over-all size and weight of the lens. Mirror lenses produce high quality pictures and are less expensive than standard lenses of comparable optical quality. Unfortunately, the mirror lens does not have a diaphragm and consequently the photographer has no choice of f stops. This limits creative options in dealing with movement or depth of field. (18)

Fast and Slow Lenses

These frequently used terms refer to the aperture size of the lens. A fast lens is able to make fast (i.e. brief) exposures because it has a large maximum aperture which permits a lot of light to enter the camera at one time. Designed to be used in dim light, fast lenses are expensive and have limited application to nature photography. A slow lens is just the opposite, requiring slow (i.e. long) exposure times because of its relatively small aperture size.

Why Change Lenses?

A camera which makes use of interchangeable lenses is of value to the nature photographer in two ways. Most obviously, it provides convenient solutions to tactical problems associated with subject magnification. A telephoto lens, for instance, permits the photographer to make a close-up portrait of a bull moose in relative safety, and a wide-angle lens will capture the panorama of a mountain range without causing the photographer to back off the edge of a cliff.

More important, using a variety of lenses expands the range of creative treatments that the photographer may apply to the subject matter, especially in dealing with perspective. (Perspective refers to the spatial relationships of the various elements of the composition, most notably the main subject and the background.) How the lens renders perspective should be the photographer's main concern when choosing a focal length. The size of the subject, which usually takes precedence over perspective in making a picture, should be controlled, when possible, by changing the camera-to-subject distance rather than the focal length of the lens. Many of the animals I have photographed could have been shot with a much shorter lens at a closer distance. However, I prefer to stay back and use a longer telephoto because of the special way the lens renders perspective.

The Normal Lens for Striking Beauty

Photographs made with a telephoto or wide-angle lens often benefit from the unusual distortion effects that characterize these lenses. By contrast the normal lens presents the scene in a natural manner and relies only on the sensitive vision of the photographer for its effect. The normal lens renders the image as if it were actually seen through the eyes of a human. As a result the picture's statement often seems more personal, and involves the viewer on a subjective level more readily than would a photograph whose technical contrivances are more apparent. **(53)**

For the nature photographer the normal lens is especially useful in photographing still life, such as landscapes, trees, fungi, or wildflowers. It makes an ideal close-up lens when used with suitable accessories.

When the beauty of a scene is strikingly apparent, the normal lens is often the most appropriate focal length. It gives the closest representation of what the photographer sees. The more extreme focal lengths are best used to accentuate or isolate beauty that may not be so obvious.

Stretching Perspective with a Wide-angle Lens

The wide-angle lens enables the photographer to work close to the subject and still get all of it in the picture. He could, for example, include a glacial stream in a composition with its mountain origin to make a statement that might be impossible with a longer lens. **(58)** The same advantage can be applied to photography inside a cave, nesting box, or other restricted spaces.

However, the photographer who thinks the wide-angle lens is the answer to spectacular scenic photography will be disappointed. It also makes the subject look smaller, and the wide expanse of a prairie or the towering immensity of a Douglas fir may appear quite insignificant if photographed with a short-focal-length lens.

Aside from solving certain tactical problems, the wide-angle lens's primary value lies in the way it renders perspective. Compared with longer focal lengths it creates an impression of expanded depth. The apparent distance between objects is increased. Near objects seem closer and distant ones seem farther away than when perceived by the eye. A close-up of an animal will reveal much more of the background than a similarly magnified image made with a lens of longer focal length. For this reason the wide-angle lens is useful in showing relationships between the subject and its environment.

The wide-angle lens achieves its most striking effect when a conscious attempt is made to distort perspective. Push a 24-mm lens into a grizzly's face and its tail will appear to be wagging in the next county. This effect is shown to best advantage by placing the camera very close to the subject matter of the foreground. **(56)**

Working with a wide-angle lens requires two special considerations. The photographer must take extra care in focusing, for at first glance in the viewfinder all parts of the scene seem to be sharp no matter where the lens is focused; however, once the film is enlarged, even small errors in focusing will be noticeable. The photographer should also be aware that vertical lines of a scene (trees for example) will lean together, or apart, in a disturbing manner if the film plane is not kept parallel to them. To change the composition without causing this distortion, the camera must be raised or lowered rather than tilted up or down.

The Intimate Aura of a Telephoto Lens

The telephoto lens allows the photographer to make detailed, intimate studies of wary creatures without the necessity of a close approach. **(5)**

Unfortunately, the telephoto does not work quite as well in practice as is popularly believed. A 500-mm lens (producing ten times more magnification than the normal lens) is about the longest focal length that is of practical use in the field, and in most cases the photographer will still need to use a blind, patient stalking or other special techniques to draw within shooting range of a wild animal. A portrait of a cottontail or blue jay, for instance, must be made at a range of five or six metres with a 500-mm optic.

Telephotos between 135 mm and 300 mm are the most useful focal lengths for nature work. Super telephotos (lenses over 500 mm) are heavy and awkward to use, and their application is limited to situations that have been well planned in advance. The more moderate focal lengths are suited for photographing birds at the nest, birds in flight, large mammals, butterflies and other large insects, reptiles and amphibians. (47)

Moderate telephotos are also used to photograph still-life subjects when the characteristic "telephoto" perspective is desired. This rendering of perspective is the opposite of that of the wide-angle lens. Space is compressed and the apparent distance between near and far objects is diminished. A photograph showing a field of wildflowers seemingly squeezed together in abnormal profusion, (16) or a landscape shot of distant hills that seem to be stacked one atop the other are products of a telephoto lens. (55) In photographs of animals this perspective lends a wild, intimate aura to the scene, as if the viewer were secretly observing the creature through a high-powered telescope.

The blurring of image detail is by far the most common technical failing of telephoto photography. This problem is almost always caused by movement or vibration of the camera during the exposure. The long lens magnifies not only the subject, it magnifies to the same degree the detrimental effects of a shaky camera. The solution is to use a tripod at all times. A pneumatic shutter release (for hands-off triggering), sand-bagging (to dampen vibrations generated inside the camera), and the use of two tripods (one under the camera and one under the lens) become more necessary as lenses get longer and shutter speeds get slower.

Buying Lenses

The photographer's first lens is usually the normal 50-mm lens that comes with the camera. Additional lenses should halve or double the existing focal lengths, and usually the photographer would want to acquire 100-mm, 200-mm, and 400-mm telephotos as well as a 24-mm wide-angle. He may wish to substitute a zoom lens for some of the fixed lenses. Such a series of lenses would meet all the needs of nature photography.

A nature photographer's equipment must withstand temperature extremes, dirt and grit, unexpected precipitation and occasional collisions with moose antlers and mountainsides. Often, photographers work in remote areas that may be days from any repair facility. Although "camera brand" lenses provide no practical optical advantage over less expensive "off-brand" lenses, they are sturdier, and more reliable. Often, good, second-hand "camera brand" lenses can be purchased inexpensively.

A final but important consideration, especially for the wildlife photographer, is the close-focusing capability of the lens. Of all wildlife subjects, ninety per cent are breadbox size or smaller and adequate magnification can usually be achieved only at the lens's minimum focusing distance. Use the 50-mm normal lens as an adequate standard. It will focus to half a metre. A 100-mm lens should then focus to one m to produce the same magnification, a 200-mm should focus to two m and so on. Long telephoto lenses in particular are likely to be unsatisfactory in this respect.

CHAPTER THREE

Shutter Speed and the Control of Motion

The camera's shutter has two functions. One is to control exposure (discussed in Section One, Chapter Five) and the other is to regulate the effect of motion, of either the subject or the camera, on the photograph being made.

Shutter speeds are calibrated so that each setting halves or doubles the speed of adjacent settings. The standard series of settings ranges from one second to 1/1000 second and includes a "B" setting which keeps the shutter open as long as the release button is depressed. Although some cameras are equipped with speeds beyond this range, the standard series is quite adequate.

A still photograph can convey the excitement of motion in different ways. The photographer can freeze the action using a fast shutter speed, or he can render a more impressionistic image by allowing the motion to register its course over the film's surface during a longer exposure.

Freezing Motion

In wildlife photography the most common use of shutter speed is to freeze action. A lion bounding over the veldt, its muscles caught in mid-ripple, or a golden eagle, wings and talons outstretched as it lands on a clifftop, are dramatic moments which pass too quickly for the eye to appreciate fully. Stop-action photography is exciting because it shows the viewer something he has never seen before—generally a successful formula for any kind of photograph. **(41)(11)(52)**

Another intriguing aspect of stop-action photography is the paradoxical manner in which it often presents the element of time. Consider a diving osprey, photographed just before it hits the water. The picture shows a bird moving at considerable speed, just about to make a spectacular splash into the drink. No matter how long we stare with anticipation at the photo, the plummeting bird never gets wet, even though everything about the picture strongly suggests the contrary. **(40)**

Stopping a Charging Moose

If it is intended that shutter speed be used to arrest all subject motion, then the photographer must consider what is about to transpire on the film surface itself, rather than the actual activity of the subject matter. Let's suppose that an adult bull moose is running directly toward the camera at top speed. Instinctively, the photographer may feel that this animal is moving quite rapidly, but a quick peek into the viewfinder reveals what will actually happen on film. The photographer sees the wide antlers, blazing eyes, flared nostrils and truncheon hooves only slowly growing larger and realizes that a moderately fast shutter speed (1/250 second) will be adequate to freeze the motion.

Alternatively, the photographer may elect to step to one side and photograph the moose as it sweeps past him. In this case the viewfinder would show a blur of animal moving into, across, and out of the frame in a flash of a second. In effect, the animal's image is traced across the film surface very rapidly, requiring a much faster shutter speed. In practice, even a speed of 1/1000 second would not be sufficient to stop this motion. **(10)**

Obviously, the direction in which the subject is moving relative to the shooting axis must be considered when the photographer is selecting an action-stopping shutter speed. He must also be aware that not all parts of the subject will necessarily be moving at the same rate or in the same direction. The shutter speed may render the moose's head satisfactorily sharp but record the hooves as unintelligible blurs. Such circumstances often produce images of exceptional power and beauty by presenting a revealing, graphic comparison of the dynamic forces at work during the exposure. **(12)**

Magnification Affects Blur

The distance which the image moves over the film's surface during exposure is determined not only by the subject's speed and direction of travel, but also by its degree of magnification. A shutter speed of 1/60 second may be sufficient to freeze the action of an entire herd of stampeding buffalo. However, a much faster speed would be required if a telephoto lens were used (or if the photographer moved closer) so that only one or two animals appeared in the frame. A hoof, whose film image may have only moved one millimetre during an exposure with a 50-mm lens, will move two mm when a more powerful 100-mm lens is used, provided exposure times are the same, and thus will appear twice as blurred.

In order to freeze action, the appropriate shutter speed is determined by considering the speed, direction and degree of magnification of the motion.

Capturing Unpredictable Action

1/Courtship of a Red-winged Blackbird

The 35-mm SLR is ideally suited for photographing wildlife when quick, unpredictable action is to be recorded. Such cameras are convenient to operate and use film which is relatively inexpensive. These factors were essential in making this photograph. After observing the blackbird for about thirty minutes, I discovered there were several distinct cattail stands which it visited regularly to display and broadcast its territorial song. I was able to place the blind with fair certainty that there would be plenty of action to shoot. Despite this advan-

tage, I was still hard-pressed to frame and focus the subject in time to catch its few seconds of display. As the bird's weight and prevailing winds caused the cattail to pitch and sway wildly at times, exposures were rattled off with a good deal of fervent hoping. However, as the camera kept firing the odds grew in my favour and by the end of the roll I had luckily come up with a picture that continues to be a favourite of mine.

Choosing an Appropriate Shutter Speed

Although later sections deal with choosing appropriate shutter speeds to stop the action of specific subjects (flying heron, running antelope, falling water, etc.), in practice this problem often resolves itself. If he is working with high-resolution colour film, the photographer should usually use the fastest shutter speed that conditions permit. However, a few general guidelines are appropriate at this point. A full-body portrait of a large herbivore engaged in activities such as walking or grazing can be made with a shutter speed of 1/60 second. Activities such as running or fighting require speeds of 1/250 second or faster. Stopping the movement of smaller animals—squirrels, weasels, birds or insects for example—will require relatively faster shutter speeds. **(3)** In general, the smaller the animal, the faster the shutter speed must be to stop its motion. A shutter speed of 1/50,000 second (not possible with stock cameras) is necessary to make a stop-action portrait of a flying grasshopper. A speed of 1/250 second will freeze almost any type of gravity-induced water movement.

Peak Action Shooting

There are several ways to improve the apparent, action-freezing properties of any shutter speed. Making the exposure at a peak or break in the action is a common method. A bird is almost motionless, but nevertheless still airborne, just prior to landing. A bumblebee hovers dead still above a blossom for an instant before zooming away. **(46)** The rise and fall of a bounding mule deer provide a shooting opportunity at the apex of each leap. By careful field observation and study of the subject's behaviour patterns, the photographer will discover many opportunities for peak-action shooting.

In many cases, the action is adequately slow, or easily predictable, so that the photographer can consciously time the shot. However, there are situations when a break in the motion does occur, but accurate timing of the exposure is nevertheless impossible. Sometimes a situation may present such exciting possibilities that the photographer is willing to waste some film in the hope of getting the shot he wants. Taking such calculated risks is a common part of nature photography.

Several years ago I was determined to get a stop-action picture of a mallard duck in flight. It had to be done in natural light and I wanted to use Kodachrome film (ASA 64). Under ideal conditions, my fastest shutter speed would be limited to 1/500 second—not nearly fast enough to freeze the movement of the wings. However, there is an instant at the top and bottom of each wingbeat when all motion stops. Armed with this simple realization, I proceeded to take several hundred close-up pictures of ducks as they flew in and out of a small pond at a city park. When I did manage to get the ducks properly framed, the bodies showed quite clearly but the wings were moving so fast that they all but disappeared. By playing the odds, I finally obtained two satisfactory pictures, one with the wings up, one with the wings down, wherein almost all motion was effectively frozen. (41)

Panning for Jackrabbit

Another way the photographer can make the best of a slow shutter speed is by tracking the motion with the camera, often called "panning". Using the viewfinder to follow a moving subject, the photographer keeps its relative position within the frame constant, thus minimizing blur. However, other elements within the frame which actually are stationary will be blurred. For example, a panning shot of a jackrabbit sprinting across the prairie will render the animal sharply but the surrounding grasses will be streaked and blurred due to the camera's movement. Images produced by this technique usually yield strong impressions of speed, yet still provide a measure of revealing, stop-action detail of the main subject. (35)

Controlling Blurred Motion

Photographers often make use of controlled blur to create images with a strong feeling of movement. Subject definition becomes secondary and in some instances may even be detrimental to the effect the photographer wishes to achieve. The blurring effect is created simply by using a shutter speed slower than that necessary to stop a subject's motion. Long exposures are used so that the movement of the image is traced over the film surface in an obvious way. (29)

With this approach, a situation rarely arises that is beyond the technical limitations of the film or shutter speed. The main challenge for the photographer is to control or otherwise anticipate the movements of the subject so that they will be recorded in a way that will yield the most dramatic effect. Even though the action may be very rapid or erratic, it is up to the photographer, as an artist, to organize these moving elements so that they will achieve maximum visual impact without losing their essential dynamic qualities. If possible, he should study the extent, speed and direction of the subject's motion carefully before choosing a shutter speed and framing the scene. Sometimes past experience is the only thing that the photographer can rely on to set up the shot.

Whether one is photographing the motion of a glacial stream, a hummingbird, or the night sky, the selection of shutter speed is critical and must be done with careful consideration to numerous factors. Relatively slow shutter speeds will give a good indication of the extent of the movement, (60) but not necessarily of its intensity or even direction—two ele-

28

Manipulating Exposure

2/Alder Grove in Pastel
The photographer seeks an exposure that aptly conveys the nature of the subject matter and his personal reaction to it. It is "correct" if it accurately communicates his intention at the time the picture was made. Before choosing an exposure setting, the photographer should decide what it is about the scene that has impressed him—shapes, textures, colour, the over-all design or some other factor. Then he can use exposure to accentuate this attractive aspect, choosing either the setting indicated by the light meter or some variation on it. As the photographer becomes familiar with the characteristics of a film, he can manipulate exposure more effectively to express his personal interpretation of a scene. The slide film from which this picture originated was given almost four times more light than was indicated by the camera's meter. The attraction of this small stand of alders was purely visual, owing to the unusual pattern created by the pastel colours and intertwining trunks and branches. Over-exposure lowered the general contrast, further softening the colour and decreasing the definition of individual trees.

29

ments that are often essential to the success of a motion photograph. The subject may become so blurred that colour intensity falls off noticeably and basic shapes lose their identity. In the extreme, recording motion with long exposures becomes an exercise in creating abstract designs whose value is unrelated to the subject matter's natural origins. At the other end of the scale, using a shutter speed that is too fast will produce a picture that is only slightly blurred, and may simply come off as a careless or technically deficient attempt at stop-action photography.

Hovering Hawks

Frequently, the movements of wildlife may be directed by the introduction of physical controls into the environment. One spring while photographing the nesting activity of marsh hawks, I decided to attempt a blurred-motion photo of an adult hawk hovering, behaviour characteristic of this species when it is hunting. However, under normal circumstances it is impossible to predict when or where this might happen. I had erected a blind near the nest site, and although the adults do not usually hover near the nest for fear of attracting attention, this location at least permitted me to draw within shooting range of my subjects. I suspected that if a foreign object were placed in the nest with the young hawks, it might deter the adult from making its usual landing. An old glove was subsequently chosen for the task and the trick worked perfectly. The female returned from hunting, spotted the glove and hovered in agitated alarm scarcely two metres above the nest on several occasions, before finally landing and removing the offensive object with her talons. In this way, I was able to exert a measure of control over the motion by limiting it to a space for which the camera had already been framed and focused and the shutter speed selected. In only three or four minutes I had exposed an entire roll of film of which a few frames aptly portrayed the marsh hawk's hovering behaviour.

Shutter Speed and the Shaky Photographer

What shutter speed is necessary to eliminate the poor image resolution that results from taking pictures with a hand-held, and thus unsteady, camera? The generally accepted answer is that the shutter speed should not be slower than the inverse of the lens focal length. For example, a shutter speed no slower than 1/50 second should be used with a 50-mm lens, a speed no slower than 1/100 second with a 100-mm lens, and so on.

This rather handy formula works for the person with average physical abilities, using average size lenses and expecting average picture sharpness. It takes into account that an increase in magnification (due to increased focal length) will result in a corresponding increase in image blur.

The formula is not valid when the photographer is using exceptionally large or heavy lenses which further aggravate his normal degree of unsteadiness. Nor is it accurate when he is using lenses in conjunction with close-up accessories, (discussed in Section One, Chapter Six) or a lens set in its "macro-focusing" mode. The photographer should also be aware that panning shots may be made at shutter speeds slower than those suggested because the fluid character of the panning action helps to eliminate the jerky vibrations that arise when he is attempting to hold the camera absolutely steady.

Although it is valuable to understand what one can get away with when hand-holding the camera, it is much more important to use a tripod—all the time!

Moving Stills

The exploration of motion by means of the still camera is in itself a fascinating endeavour of unlimited possibilities. The nature photographer carries the process one step further and attempts to deal with motion in terms of its relationship to living forms and other natural phenomena.

Close-ups
of the Bizarre
and Beautiful

3/Locomotion Across a Leaf
*Effective close-up images are generally
the result of more preparation, planning,
and technical discipline than those
made at normal working distances. This
picture of a spider mincing across a leaf
was made with a 50-mm lens, bellows
and two small electronic flash units
attached to the front of the lens. The
short flash duration (1/1000 second)
produced a sharp image even though the
camera was hand-held. The intensity of
the light permitted the use of a small
aperture which increased the depth of
field, making focusing easier. In-camera
magnification was about two × life size.*

4/Male Polyphemus Moth

To tame this bizarre-looking beast, I cooled it off in the refrigerator for about twenty minutes. While the giant moth (wingspan fifteen cm) was calming down, I prepared a small, natural-looking photographic set using a few oak leaves, and placed it on my sun porch. (The day was overcast.) The camera was equipped with a bellows, 100-mm lens, and cable release and was mounted on a tripod. I carefully framed the prepared stage and fixed the exposure settings by taking a through-the-lens meter reading of the natural light reflected from a grey card held at the subject position (f 11 at 1/8 second with Kodachrome 64). Preparations completed, the lethargic insect was brought to the set. In about fifteen minutes the pictures were made and the animal was again ready for the wilds, fluttering off to resume its search for a mate as soon as I released it.

CHAPTER FOUR

Aperture and Depth of Field

There are two reasons for adjusting the aperture size of a lens. One is to regulate exposure (discussed in Section One, Chapter Five) and the other is to control depth of field.

The size of the aperture, or lens opening, is adjusted by turning a ring, on the outside of the lens barrel, which is linked to an inner diaphragm constructed of sliding, overlapping metal leaves. Like the iris of the eye, the diaphragm can open up or close down to regulate the passage of light. Aperture settings are called "f stops," and range in size from f1.0 (the largest) to f45 or even smaller. The f stop settings of a normal 50-mm lens are usually f2, f2.8, f4, f5.6, f8, f11, f16. Progressing along this scale, each aperture setting is only half the size of the preceding one.

Depth of Field

Depth of field is a photographic term that refers to the amount or extent of a scene which appears to be in focus. Depth of field is minimal when only a narrow band or plane of sharpness is evident in a photograph. **(31)** Maximum depth of field occurs when the photograph is sharp from foreground to background.

Depth of field extends farther behind the point at which the lens is actually focused than it does in front. This inequity increases with shorter-focal-length lenses and at greater focal distances.

Accomplished photographers give careful attention to depth of field in deciding both its extent and where it will be placed in the scene. For a nature photographer involved in creative work, it is always a primary consideration.

Magnification Sets the Limits
Whether one is photographing Hell's Canyon or the fanged jaws of a wolf spider, depth of field is ultimately determined by how much the scene is

magnified. Magnification is one of the first and most important considerations in designing an image. It increases when the photographer uses a more powerful lens or moves closer to the subject. As the magnification increases, the depth of field decreases. **(59)(39)**

Adjustments to the depth of field are almost invariably made after the lens focal length and camera-to-subject distance are established. Within these limits the photographer is able to control the depth of field by adjusting the lens aperture.

Aperture Size Regulates Depth of Field

In practice, the photographer thinks about and manipulates depth of field in terms of aperture size. This relationship is simple: as aperture size is made smaller, depth of field increases.

Consider the application of this principle to making a photograph of an eared grebe, a robin-sized water bird. **(44)** A 500-mm lens will be used to avoid approaching the animal too closely. To achieve adequate magnification, a camera-to-subject distance of about four metres will be required. With the lens aperture at f5.6, depth of field is about two centimetres. Stopped down to the smallest aperture of f32, the depth of field increases to about twelve cm.

Grebe in a Haystack

The photographer can elect to use any depth of field between these two extremes. Obviously, an unpredictable, moving subject like a grebe calls for the use of maximum depth of field to compensate for the errors in focusing that are bound to occur. However, if the photographer is using fine-grained colour film (ASA 64), the fastest possible shutter speed that can be used with the f32 setting under the brightest natural light is 1/15 of a second. Although this speed might be suitable for a blurred motion picture, it is far too slow to produce a detailed rendering of the subject.

The Depth-of-Field Dilemma

Suppose the photographer opts for a faster shutter speed. To compensate for the light lost, a larger aperture must be used. Consequently depth of field decreases, leaving less margin for focusing error. This is not a great problem if the subject is stationary. However, with a moving subject like a grebe, the photographer finds once again that obtaining a satisfactorily sharp image is not easy. **(37)**

High-resolution (finely detailed) images of active subjects require the use of fast shutter speeds and small apertures—conditions not suited to the use of fine-grained colour film. Usually the photographer is forced to favour one factor at the expense of the other, the choice being governed by

Revealing Glimpses
with a Telephoto Lens

5/Black Bear in the Underbrush
*Under natural conditions black bears are
dispersed over a wide area and seldom
encounter one another. This picture was
made near a rural dump which had
drawn together a considerable number
of bears. The quarrelsome, close-quarter
feeding was evidenced by the scars and
seeping wounds carried by many of the
animals. One older bear, in obviously
poor condition, had become overly bold
around humans, taking advantage of
their presence to feed while the other
bears fled into the underbrush. This was
a hazardous situation for photography;
there were so many bears hidden in the
dense vegetation that if one strayed too
far from the vehicle, it was easy to be
cut off unknowingly from a safe retreat,
a special worry due to the presence of
sows with cubs. Further, the bears
would carry their spoils into the bush to
feed and so became very possessive of
their territory. A telephoto lens was
needed to maintain a safe working
distance. This portrait shows the
intimate, wild aura typical of photographs made with a very long lens (in
this case 500 mm). With so much of the
picture's effect being dependent on the
bear's head, it was necessary that it be
rendered as sharply as possible. Like
most of the photographs in the book, it
was made with a sturdy tripod and a
pneumatic shutter release.*

the constraints of the moment. Often the ambient light is so weak that both shutter speed and aperture size have to be compromised.

There are other ways of dealing with this problem. A high-speed film may be used. This permits the use of faster shutter speeds and smaller apertures but yields photographs of lower image resolution due to the film's coarse grain. (13) Another common way of getting around the problem is to intensify the light by using an electronic flash. This method produces sharp, finely detailed images. However, such pictures almost always appear contrived. Obvious artificial illumination in a nature photograph is certainly less than ideal, and to some people even offensive, but with active subjects requiring high magnification (insects, small birds) the use of electronic flash is the only way to obtain readable, stop-action pictures. (15)

No field of photography presents such formidable technical constraints as those encountered by nature photographers working with active, wild subjects in existing light. A newspaper photographer loads his Nikon with high-speed black and white film (ASA 1600), sets the shutter at 1/1000 of a second, the aperture at f16 and blasts away with little cause to worry about inadequate depth of field or subject motion. Photographers working in studios have complete control not only of their subject matter, but also of the intensity and direction of the lighting. Of the many critical factors involved in making a wildlife photograph, inducing a wary animal to venture into a depth-of-field zone of decidedly limited extent is one of the greatest challenges. (49) Variations on this dilemma are encountered whether one is photographing a hungry caterpillar, a wind-jostled orchid or a prowling cougar.

However, when the nature photographer works with inanimate subject matter, restriction of depth of field is no longer a concern. With few or no technical limitations generated by the subject on the choosing of lens focal length, shutter speed or aperture, there is far more latitude in setting the depth of field. For the photographer it becomes a creative tool of considerable artistic import. (27)

The Preview Button

The extent and placement of the sharpness zone may be precisely judged by the use of the depth-of-field preview button found on single-lens reflex cameras. Normally, the lens aperture remains wide open to permit bright, easy focusing until the shutter is activated. The preview button allows the lens to be stopped down to shooting aperture any time the photographer wishes to examine the depth of field.

When the lens is stopped down at small apertures, the viewfinder may appear to black out. Viewing will be much improved if the eyepiece is shielded from stray light by a rubber eyecup, and the photographer waits a few moments for his vision to adjust to the lower light level.

Sharpening a Heron's Beak

The preview button is important in obtaining top quality images. When composing a picture, the photographer usually focuses on the centre of interest. However, if the centre of interest is comprised of more than one element, or there are a number of secondary elements of nevertheless critical importance, the lens should be focused so that the depth-of-field zone encompasses all such elements. (4) A picture of a great blue heron would be less than satisfactory if the photographer focused on the eyes and allowed the depth of field to extend wastefully into the air behind the bird. Previewing the depth of field would allow the photographer to make a slight readjustment in focusing to bring both the eyes and the long beak into the zone of sharpness.

The preview button is just as important in work with still-life subjects. The lack of movement means that aperture, rather than shutter speed, becomes a priority, and as a result the photographer is afforded a wide range of depths of field from which to choose. This can only be done effectively with the preview button, which allows the photographer to see and compare the relative effect of each depth on the image.

Stretching the Depth of Field

The apparent extent of the depth-of-field zone may be improved if care is taken to keep the camera and, at close-up range, the actual film plane, equidistant from important elements. A simplistic application would be to make a profile shot of a rhinoceros rather than shooting from a frontal or oblique angle. This approach places the camera equidistant from both horn and tail, producing satisfactory results with minimal depth of field.

When doing close-up studies, the photographer no longer thinks in terms of the camera, but rather in terms of the 24 x 36-mm section of film that is recording the image. Suppose the subject is two tiny wildflowers. Magnification is life size and depth of field seems almost non-existent. By adjustments of only a few millimetres, the photographer tilts and repositions the camera back (i.e. film plane) until both blossoms are equidistant from their respective sections of the film. Naturally, all of this fine tuning is done with an eye to the viewfinder.

Some manufacturers offer close-up bellows attachments which permit the photographer to tilt and shift the camera back independently of the lens. Normally, the depth-of-field zone is fixed at right angles to the camera-subject axis, but a bellows allows the photographer to run the depth of field through the composition at a variety of angles. Thus, depth

Delicate Tones and Subtle Light

6/Winter Starling
Introduced into North America in the late nineteenth century, the starling has since extended its range over most of the continent. To the dismay of many bird lovers its rapid success has been at the expense of native species which share its nesting requirements—the flicker, bluebird and great-crested flycatcher. Nevertheless, it is a handsome animal.

During the winter it is easily drawn to backyard feeders and the bird pictured is probing for suet stuffed into the log. The lighting is a combination of fill-in flash and low, winter sun. The impression-istic mood is partly because I framed the picture with the camera tilted at a 45° angle which made the sun appear to be hitting the scene from below.

7/Rufous Hummingbird at a
Flowering Red Currant Bush
*The catchlight in this tiny bird's eye
gives a good idea of where the sun was
located when the picture was taken—
almost directly overhead. Usually,
midday lighting does not produce
pleasing results but in this case, two
factors were in my favour. Most of the
foliage surrounding the bird was struck
by light diffused by the vegetation
growing overhead which lowered the
contrast in the background, softening
and enriching the colours. This effect
was intensified by the shallow depth of
field produced by a telephoto lens (500
mm with extension tube), and by
framing the scene to make the most of
the surrounding colour.*

of field may be placed with far greater effectiveness without the necessity of altering the composition as would happen in the previous example. Special purpose, perspective-control (PC) lenses, commonly used in architectural photography but also valuable for scenic work, in the same way permit a more effective use of depth of field at normal distances.

The Depth-of-Field Scale

The depth-of-field scale engraved on the lens barrel serves as a general guide in determining the extent of the depth of field at various apertures and distances. Its primary value lies in providing data helpful in presetting the lens for situations where last-minute focusing is impossible, such as in remote control or fast action work.

Focusing for Greatest Depth

The depth-of-field scale also indicates at what distance the lens should be focused to provide the greatest depth at a given aperture. Such a depth of field would stretch from infinity to some nearer point. (57) Suppose a photographer wishes to record a mountain scene in complete sharpness from distant peaks to the alpine wildflowers at his feet. The aperture is selected—in this case f16 to maximize depth of field. Then the focusing ring is turned so that the infinity mark lies opposite the f16 mark on the depth-of-field scale. The other f16 mark on the depth-of-field scale will then be opposite a mark on the distance scale that will indicate the near limit of the depth of field. Of course, the actual focused distance (called in photographic jargon the "hyperfocal distance") is somewhere between the near and far limit of the depth of field. Using this setting, the photographer then frames the scene with care to exclude elements in front of the depth-of-field zone. This method of setting the lens at the hyperfocal distance may be used for any aperture incorporated in the scale.

CHAPTER FIVE

Light and Film

The sun has a special symbolic significance to the nature photographer. Its light energy powers the basic photosynthetic process that culminates in the fiery hues of an oak-hickory forest, the dark, sinewy bulk of a killer whale or the flashing wings of a peregrine. However, the sun is not only mother of the fascinating life forms that become subject matter for the lens; it is of course the essence of photography itself. Sunlight or, in most cases, reflected sunlight, in its many variations, is the cause and controller of the chemical reaction that results in a photographic image.

Several characteristics of light are particularly important to creative photography. Most notable of these are the relative intensity of the light and its angle of incidence on the subject. Many novice photographers direct too much attention to choosing subject matter, lens focal length or camera angle, neglecting to develop a basic awareness of how light affects the image. Gaining a sensitivity to the special photographic qualities of light is not difficult, but for the beginner it requires a novel shift in everyday habits of perception. Conscious effort and practice are necessary to see the light that reflects from the subject rather than the subject itself. Photographers need to retrain their visual outlook to notice such aspects as the shadows on the underside of a roast turkey or the reflective properties of a glistening lip. One must generally try to see the world with a perception untainted by human prejudice, developing the detached impartial vision of a light-recording machine. Ironically, by gaining fluency in the impersonal language of light and film one is more able to communicate subjective views and feelings through photography.

Judging Light Quality

The over-all brightness of a scene can be measured accurately with a light meter and after a little practice and experience the photographer can produce satisfactory exposures with some confidence. The light falling on the

Improving the Natural Light

8/Skipper on a Thistle

A wildlife photographer needs to develop an alertness for picture opportunities. Usually they pass quickly and are seldom repeated. It was not difficult to notice the steady stream of skipper butterflies that visited this thistle patch in my backyard. On several occasions I perched on a campstool beside them, soaking up sun and following the activity of the small insects through the camera's viewfinder. Although the shadows of this photograph are well illuminated, careful examination will reveal that the picture was made when the sun was almost directly overhead. The stark lighting normally expected at this time of day was softened by the use of fill-in flash. With this technique it is desirable that the effect of the flash be inconspicuous and not overpower the natural light.

9/Yellow Pine Chipmunk
Although shot under midday lighting conditions, this picture shows only moderate contrast, with good detail remaining in the shadow regions. The chipmunk was attracted by a natural food source that had been laced with peanut butter. To improve the lighting conditions, I manoeuvred the small rodent onto a brightly coloured rock that acted as a reflector, bouncing light into the animal's underparts.

scene, in combination with the reflective properties of the subject matter itself, results in the subject's brightness. However, in most cases, the quality of the light is just as important as its over-all intensity and the photographer's ability to judge its pictorial effect is crucial to the picture-making process.

Hard Light
Light quality has a direct bearing on the relative brightness of various elements of the scene. At one extreme is light that photographers call "hard" or "specular." This is the type of light emitted by a point light source like the sun, an electronic flash unit or a bare, clear light bulb. The light generated travels in clean, parallel waves and upon striking an object casts sharp, well-defined shadows. Sunlight attains this harsh, spotlight-like quality most acutely when the sun is directly overhead on a cloudless day. (47) Such light accentuates the differences in brightness of the subject and increases the apparent contrast of these tones. Shadows appear exceedingly dark and abrupt while subject highlights are brilliant. (52) This great contrast, or range, in subject brightness is often impossible to record accurately on colour film. If exposure is set to give a faithful recording of the highlight, the shadows turn black and lose detail. Should the approach be reversed to give exposure priority to the shadows, the highlight will be washed out, losing colour and detail.

The ability of a photographic emulsion to cope with such contrast in subject brightness is called "film latitude". Great latitude of course is highly desirable, but unfortunately no colour film has yet been produced that can record the light intensity ratios of one thousand to one that are sometimes encountered on a sunny day. It is left to the photographer then to devise ways of lowering or otherwise coping with this high-contrast lighting in a way that suits the film's capabilities.

Soft Light
"Soft" or "diffuse" light has properties opposite to those just discussed. Usually it originates from a source of illumination that is partially obscured from the subject. Parallel waves of sunlight, for instance, are broken and deflected in a variety of directions on passing through a layer of cloud. Hence, the shadows they cast are soft and indistinct, and on overcast days may be almost indiscernible. This type of light illuminates the subject evenly, creating little contrast in the relative brightness of the scene. For this reason film can more easily record the narrow range of tones that this lighting affords. Technically it is the most fitting type of light for photography. (61)(19)

Count Clouds for Appealing Light

On sunny days photographers can notice an immediate difference in the starkness of shadows as white clouds begin to gather in the sky. Although the sun continues to shine directly on the scene, shadows are softened by the light that is deflected into them from the under-surface of the clouds, as well as by the light that is scattered on passing through the cloud layer. Contrast in subject brightness is lessened, and stronger, more saturated, colour reproduction is achieved by the film.

Contrast decreases dramatically once the sun is obscured by cloud, mist, fog or a canopy of leaves. In effect, the low-contrast light neutralizes the high-contrast aspects of the subject matter. The even illumination permits the film to register the full effect of each colour, none being blocked or washed out by improper exposure. Subjects with an inherently narrow contrast range, such as an earthworm lying in the soil, to cite an extreme example, may gain little photogenic benefit from low-contrast light. It is left to artistic judgement to make appropriate combinations of light and subject matter.

The Drama of Dawn and Dusk

The appealing quality of diffuse light attains its dramatic apex, and certainly its greatest favour with photographers in general, at dawn and dusk. (53) This early morning or late afternoon light is seasoned by a number of natural factors. The low angle of the sun means that its rays travel a greater distance through the atmosphere and thus are subject to far more diffusion by minute airborne particles than is light from a midday sun, which follows a direct, perpendicular course to the earth. Due to the angles involved, clouds, if present, can soften the light further by bouncing illumination back into the shadows. When the sun is just below the horizon and does not cast direct illumination on the subject, its light may nevertheless be reflected onto the scene from the clouds overhead. This particular situation occurs rarely but the light produced has a delicate quality that can lend exquisite beauty to an otherwise commonplace scene. (62)

Beware of Image Contrast

The contrast or relative brightness of a photographic image depends partly on the reflective properties of the subject and partly on the quality of the illumination. The photographer must develop a sensitivity to this crucial aspect of picture making. (9) Due to the inability of film, especially colour film, to record a wide range of reflected light levels, some diffusion of the light source is generally preferable. Every photographer has had the experience of photographing an exciting subject under midday sunlight only to be disappointed with the quality of the developed images due to the harsh

Preparations for Fast Action

10/American Widgeon Taking Flight
The explosive energy that can catapult a one-kg duck straight up from the water with scarcely a twitch of warning is amazing. The widgeon is actually into the second downward thrust of its wings. The first is made against the water itself and serves to launch the duck. Observation of the take-off habits of birds allowed me to frame this scene accurately long before the bird took to the air. Even at 1/500 of a second the motion of the bird becomes blurred only a split second after take-off.

11/Rearing Grizzly

Water can be a great asset to any nature photograph. It is, of course, one of life's basic elements and, like the sun, is of special significance to the naturalist. From a photographic standpoint, it catches the least glimmer of light and can take on an infinite variety of shape and colour. In this photograph it provides a visual record of the bear's movements, adding sparkle and dynamism to the portrait, as well as infusing the image with a sense of immediacy. While I was resting quietly beside a stream, the grizzly arrived unannounced and started across. Luckily, the camera was correctly adjusted for the lighting conditions, and was beside me on a tripod. Simple expediency dictated that I shoot first and check the settings later. The sound of the first exposure caused the animal to pause and then stand up. A few seconds after this picture was taken, both of us left, in opposite directions.

lighting. To illustrate this point, consider an exception to the usual situation—the abnormally compelling quality of pictures of skiers photographed beneath a clear, noon sun. On closer examination the reason for the success of these images is obvious. Despite the negative effect of the specular light source, they succeed due to the excellent reflective properties of the snow which bounces light into the shadows and provides rich, vibrant colour rendition. **(48)**

Light Has Colour

Light also has another characteristic of importance to the photographer—colour. Sunlight is composed of all visible wavelengths of light, each wavelength producing what we see as a characteristic colour on striking a substance that reflects it. If a wavelength is absorbed we do not see its colour. If all wavelengths are absorbed we see black, and if all are reflected the substance appears white. Daylight may vary considerably in its colour composition due to atmospheric particles which absorb, or filter out, certain wavelengths. **(61)(21)** The warm, yellow-orange hues of light that are encountered early or late in the day result from an absence of blue wavelengths. When the sun is directly overhead it has cooler, more evenly balanced properties. If the sky is overcast the colour of the light is also evenly balanced but shows little variation between sun-up and sun-down.

Direction of Light

Light may strike a scene from a variety of directions. Its angle of incidence on the subject affects exposure selection as well as the visual and emotional impact of the image itself. Thus, the angle of illumination becomes a routine but critical concern for the photographer. Although directional lighting is discussed here in several separate categories, the transition from one to the next is gradual.

Frontlighting for Shape and Colour

Frontlighting occurs when the sun is behind the photographer, casting illumination onto the parts of the subject that face the camera. **(45)** Usually it makes for easy exposure determination because all parts of the scene are equally lit. Due to the absence of shadows, frontlight is not suitable for portraying depth, interesting textures or three-dimensional shapes. However, it is appropriate when the photographer's primary aim is to show shape, such as the natural surface patterns and graceful outline of a butterfly's wing. **(24)** Due to its direct, even illumination, frontlight is best for situations requiring a strong, pure expression of colour.

   The flatness of frontlighting also lends an intriguing, surreal quality to scenes with strong perspective elements that do not depend on colour or shadow, such as converging parallel lines. This juxtaposition of flat lighting with strongly three-dimensional graphic elements presents an image that attains dynamism by virtue of these contradictory factors, producing an impression of simultaneous expansion and contraction.

Sidelighting for Texture and Form

As the term suggests, sidelighting strikes the scene at right angles to the camera-to-subject axis. The shadows cast by this oblique lighting reveal the subject's texture. Sidelight also enhances form. The strong contrast produced by shadow and highlight surfaces helps to define the different planes of a subject and show its three-dimensional aspects.

From a graphic standpoint, sidelight increases the number of tonal variations due to the differing light intensities striking the subject. Noticeable shadows contrast markedly with highlights of the scene. This increase in picture elements means that composition becomes relatively more complicated than it would be with frontlighting. Thus, the strong visual impact of sidelighting is generally used to best effect when other picture elements (lines, shapes, colour) are kept simple.

Exposure is determined quite subjectively when colour slide film, in particular, is being used. As the highlights and shadows cannot both be satisfactorily exposed at the same time, due to the film's narrow latitude, the photographer must decide which will receive priority, or if a compromise exposure is the best solution. Black and white film not only has more exposure latitude to begin with, it also allows the photographer more direct control over developing and printing, which permits easier accommodation of the high-contrast effects of sidelighting.

Backlighting for Mood and Silhouette

Backlighting is used by many photographers for establishing mood. This lighting originates behind the subject, and like the other types of directional lighting discussed it varies in degree. The camera side of the subject is not illuminated except for a thin halo of light around the edges. If the subject matter is somewhat translucent, such as a bird's wing, a raindrop or a leaf, the backlight will project through, lending the subject an apparent luminosity of its own. (30) Even with considerable experience it is not easy to previsualize the effect of backlighting on the picture.

The reason for the strong mood, or appeal to emotion, that backlighting evokes is best judged in context of the over-all image. However, in general, the bare outline or suggestion of the physical mass of a subject produced by the halo lighting effect tends to carry the viewer's consciousness beyond the simple reality of the photograph itself. (26) If exposure priority, and thus detail, is given to the shadow portion of the scene, the subject's outline becomes over-exposed, loses definition and takes on a

Expressing
the Sensation
of Motion

12/Heron Shaking Prey
The most interesting aspect of this image is the way the film, exposed at a shutter speed of 1/125 of a second, has recorded the various movements of the water, fish and bird. The great blue heron, intent on catching its dinner, was aware of my approach but refused to be scared away until its task was accom-plished. I was positioned to make the picture of the bird as it lunged character-istically into the water for the fish. Once the prey was seized, however, the heron turned immediately away from the camera, a story told by the water's turbulence. Fortunately, its movement caused the scene to be framed in a way that captured the major part of the spraying liquid. As evidenced in this picture, airborne water droplets, backlit by a low sun, show up dramatically when shot against a dark background.

similar surreal quality. Backlighting is the most abstract type of illumination, rendering the scene in a way we seldom experience it because of our tendency to interpret visual stimuli in terms of how the mind expects it to appear. Human vision can also accommodate, more readily than film, backlighting's wide range of light intensities.

The great contrast involved in backlighting means that obtaining the desired exposure requires extra care. Light meter readings vary tremendously depending on which part of the scene is being measured. Normal exposure precautions are necessary, including bracketing and close-up metering of the subject, which are both discussed more fully later in this chapter.

Another problem which often occurs with backlighting is lens flare, caused when sunlight shines directly into the lens. It can be lessened by using a proper lens hood, or eliminated by choosing a different camera angle. However, flare is not necessarily a technical flaw and may often be put to artistic advantage. Keep in mind that the amount of flare increases as the aperture size increases. Its effect can be judged accurately with the camera's depth-of-field preview mechanism.

Exposure Basics

Achieving accurate film exposure is not difficult provided the photographer's approach remains compatible with the principles on which the equipment and film were designed. It's comforting to know that each roll of film has a built-in margin for exposure error. Colour slide film will continue to produce satisfactory results if under-exposed or over-exposed by 1½ stops, and colour print film or black and white film will tolerate considerably more error.

Film is sensitive to differences in light intensity and responds correctly to a relatively narrow and unchangeable level of brightness. Whether the subject is a sun-drenched beach or a moonlit winter forest, a particular film will require roughly the same amount of light in each situation to produce a satisfactory image.

Exposure is controlled by selecting a combination of shutter speed and aperture that allows the entry of an amount of light compatible with the sensitivity of the film. The photographer has the choice of letting in a lot of light quickly (large aperture/fast shutter speed) or allowing a small quantity of light to trickle in for a greater period of time (small aperture/slow shutter speed), or any combination in between.

Think Like a Light Meter
The most demanding aspect of exposure is interpreting the readings provided by the light meter. First of all one must keep in mind which specific

areas of the scene are being measured. Some through-the-lens meters make an average reading of the entire frame; others measure a small, clearly defined, central spot. The most popular metering system incorporates a centre-weighted design which gives priority to the centre of the frame with sensitivity decreasing toward the edges.

The photographer must keep in mind not only how his particular light meter is measuring the scene, but also that it works on the principle that everything is grey. Regardless of type or brand of meter, all are designed to produce exposure information for an average subject, which in photographic parlance is neutral grey and reflects eighteen per cent of the light striking it. Fortunately this arrangement works unusually well for most situations in which the nature photographer finds himself.

Light Meter Causes Wild Bear Mutations
Point a light meter at a polar bear, and it will indicate an exposure which, if followed precisely, will yield an image of a bear that is grey rather than Arctic white. The light meter thinks the bruin is merely a grey object under bright light rather than a white object under somewhat dimmer illumination. Both situations would cause the same reading. Realizing this, the photographer may let in more light (in this case probably one stop) to make sure the bear comes out white. Preferably, he could take a reading of something that actually is grey, or of average brilliance, provided it is being illuminated in the same fashion as the bear, and use this data to set the exposure. **(50)**

Similar problems will result if the photographer uses a reading taken directly from an extremely dark subject like a black bear. In this case "grey bear" can be avoided by decreasing the exposure one or two stops from the light meter's indicated setting or, preferably, using exposure data gleaned from a similarly illuminated subject of average brilliance. Although special care must be taken when determining exposure for subjects that are exceptionally light or dark, little trouble will arise if the limitations of the light meter are taken into consideration by the photographer.

Exposure Priority for Centre of Interest
Taking meter readings is a straightforward process for scenes that have average or low contrast. However, high-contrast scenes for which a light meter will register a difference of more than three stops between light areas and dark areas, require more care. The photographer will want the most important part of the scene to be exposed correctly to show maximum detail and accurate colour. **(24)(23)** The common procedure is to take a close-up meter reading so that only light from the centre of interest is measured, before moving back to the picture-taking position. Sometimes it is advisable to moderate such a reading by one stop in favour of

Soft Images
for Special Moods

13/Migrating Canada Geese
A skein of geese moving against the sky seldom fails to evoke a long, wistful look from an earthbound human. For a few seconds our thoughts fly after the birds, chasing a richer world waiting just over the horizon. For the bird, migration is its greatest adventure and its greatest peril—from storms, hunger, fatigue, hunters and confused navigation. Many species travel after dark, finding their way by the moon and stars. In this photograph the moon's great size is the product of a 1000-mm telephoto lens. Sharpness is not always an asset to a picture. After dark we experience a normal decrease in visual acuity. Thus, the softness of this image, resulting from the coarse grain of a high-speed film, is appropriate, and also lends a romantic mood to the scene.

the areas of secondary importance. Such close-up metering procedures are accomplished more easily by a spot meter than by the averaging type. Of course, with many wildlife subjects a close approach is not possible, but a telephoto lens may be mounted to obtain a more discriminating exposure reading, and then exchanged for the focal length required for the actual picture-making.

Creative Juggling of Exposure Settings

Once the base exposure is decided, it is a simple procedure to move to a new combination of aperture and shutter speed that may be more suitable to the creative or technical aims of the photographer. Suppose, for example, the light meter indicates an exposure of f16 at 1/60 second to photograph a bumblebee foraging over a dandelion. Wishing to use a faster shutter speed to ensure that camera movement does not affect the sharpness of the image, the photographer increases the speed by three stops to 1/500 second. To compensate for the loss of light this causes, he merely opens up the aperture by three stops to f5.6. With a little practice such manipulation of f stop and shutter speed becomes as easy as dodging a set of moose antlers.

Reciprocity Failure

When exposure times exceed one or two seconds, film ceases to behave typically. Unless corrections are made, the resulting photographs will suffer from under-exposure and unpredictable shifts in colour balance—an effect called "reciprocity failure." Precise correction of these inconsistencies varies with each film type. However, a simple rule of thumb is to increase exposure by one stop when the shutter speed called for is between two seconds and fifteen seconds, and by two stops for any shutter speed that is longer. Reciprocity failure is seldom a factor in nature photography unless one is working in a shaded forest at small apertures using a lens extension device; in this instance shutter speed can frequently exceed two seconds, especially if a slow colour film is used. Such a situation is most likely to be encountered in photographing fungi and lichens.

Practical Suggestions

In practice, the camera's through-the-lens light meter works extremely well. Rarely have I found a hand-held light meter to be of value. Here are a few more suggestions for dealing with exposure:

- BRACKETING—When confronted with a tricky lighting situation I bracket exposures. This is simply a systematic process of taking some extra pictures in the hope that at least one will turn out. Usually it is sufficient to vary the base exposure by one full stop over as well as under, although in crucial situations the photographer may want to extend the process.

- THE GREY CARD—Most of the time I carry in my pocket a folded-up, photographic grey card, sold in camera stores. This card reflects eighteen per cent of the light hitting it and is the perfect "average" subject for a light meter. Held close in front of the lens so that it is struck by the same light hitting the subject, it assists in determining exposure for high contrast and extremely light or dark subjects.

- THE f16 RULE—I use this easy-to-remember rule whenever I am working outside to double-check light meter readings and generally make sure I'm playing in the right ball park. It works like this: under sunny conditions the aperture should be set at f16 and the shutter speed should be set to correspond with the ASA rating of the film. For example, with Kodachrome 64 (ASA 64) the settings would be f16 at 1/64 second (or whatever shutter speed is closest). Open the aperture to f11 if it's lightly overcast, another stop if it seems about to pour alligators, and a further stop if the subject is in the shade on a sunny day. This series of exposure settings is identical to the recommendations that accompany every roll of film.

Know One Film Well

When doing nature photography I use but one kind of film in almost all situations. As opposed to shooting with a variety of film types, this practice has enabled me to gain a much better understanding of a particular emulsion and in turn a greater control over the image-making process. I am familiar with the film's reaction to different kinds of light and colour, with its capacity for sharpness under various conditions, and perhaps most important, I am able to judge its exposure requirements even without the aid of a light meter. The advice is simple: spend enough time to find a film that matches your needs and aspirations in nature photography, and then, within reason, use it exclusively.

Colour or Black and White

Unfortunately, the attractive characteristics of black and white film can only be fully exploited with sheet film, so that individual negatives may be specially exposed, developed and printed to satisfy each picture-making attempt. These procedures are not possible with the roll-film cameras used so extensively for nature photography. For many years black and white film was the only kind available and photographers painstakingly carted their heavy view cameras up mountainsides and across swollen streams. Even today the black and white genre continues to have a strong following but the number of adherents diminishes steadily as nature photographers in general become enamoured of the greater excitement and potential of colour film. Of the various psychological components that comprise our sense of vision, colour is one of the strongest, particularly in eliciting emotional response. Consider further that much of the earth's natural beauty rests in the simple but infinitely varied spectacle of its colour. It doesn't make sense to me to use a film that is blind to an element which we find so fascinating, and to which we are by nature so keenly sensitive.

Prints or Slides

Deciding whether to use print or slide film is not difficult for the serious photographer. Consider the following points:

- Slide film is capable of producing images with finer detail and richer, more accurate colour than print film.
- Slides can not only be projected for an audience, they can also be made into sharp, brilliant prints at least equal to those made with negative film, although the cost is somewhat greater.
- Slide film is less expensive and thus better suited for photographing wild, active subjects where film wastage is to be expected.
- With few exceptions publishers use only slides for colour reproduction. Although making photographs worthy of publication may seem like a distant proposition to a beginning photographer, it becomes more feasible when one considers that much of the nature photography published is done by amateurs.

ASA Rating: High Speed *vs* Fine Grain

Film is manufactured in various degrees of sensitivity to light. In North America, film sensitivity is measured in ASA (American Standards Association) code numbers. In Canada, ASA numbers are often referred to as ISO (International Standards Organization) numbers. **(45)** The more sensitive a film is to light the higher is its film speed or ASA number. When the sensitivity of a film doubles, its ASA number also doubles. Under identical circumstances a film of ASA 100 (or ISO 100) would allow the use of a shutter speed one stop faster, or an aperture one stop smaller, than a film of ASA 50.

High-speed film has the advantage of allowing the use of fast shutter speeds to stop action, and small apertures for increased depth of field. Naturally these characteristics are highly desirable to the nature photographer. **(13)** Nevertheless, in most situations they fail to compensate for the benefits gained from using a slower film. Lower-speed films are finer

Electronic Flash for Nocturnal Creatures

14/Painted Turtle

This portrait was illuminated by one electronic flash unit, hand-held above and out to the side of the camera. The light was softened by placing a layer of Kleenex over the flash reflector. When making sidelit portraits I try to position the flash so that the animal is looking into the light. This lends an openness to the image and usually means the most interesting part of the animal is well illuminated. This picture was made with the assistance of my seven-year-old nephew, who supplied the subject, and, as my hands were full of equipment, also kept it under control. Some of the kids in my neighbourhood know a modest reward awaits them for information leading to the location of a bird nest, squirrel den, snake or even a nice bug. A little advertising occasionally leads to some easy and interesting discoveries.

15/Dangling Tree Frog

Sticky toe pads of the tiny Pacific tree frog allow it to cling to small bits of vegetation. This specimen was photographed in a bouquet of grasses sitting on my kitchen table. As the animal clambered about I merely turned the container to bring it back into photographic position. Two small electronic flashes were attached to the front of the lens with adjustable brackets, and provide the even illumination for this nocturnal amphibian. A 100-mm macro lens and extension bellows were used to produce an in-camera magnification close to life size.

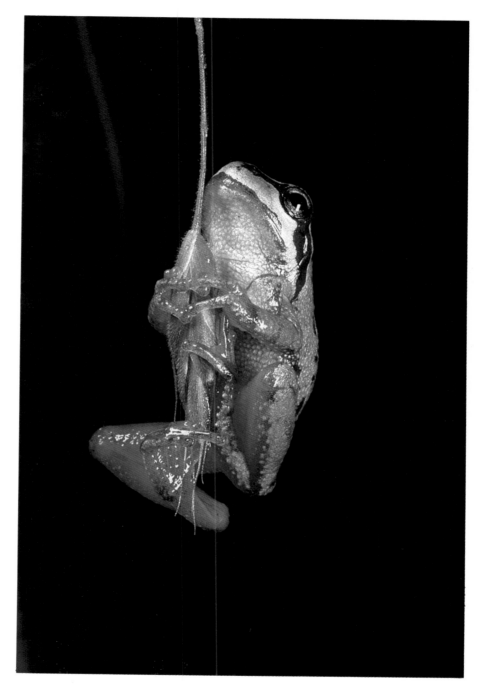

grained, producing images of higher resolution and improved detail. In general they are also lower in contrast and give richer, more saturated colour.

The film speed a photographer chooses is often a matter of personal taste. Slower film always has the potential to produce an image of superior technical quality. On the other hand, a fast film may occasionally be the only way of obtaining any recognizable image at all. Occasionally I will resort to faster film (above ASA 100) for special situations such as shooting birds in flight under natural light.

Filtering the Light

Inexpensive and easily attached to the front of the lens, filters are used for a variety of reasons. Some, called "special effect" filters, produce images with artificial adornments—highlights that look like starbursts, images that are repeated kaleidoscope-fashion within a single frame, and scenes framed by a romantic mist, or worse, the outline of a keyhole. Most of these filters are clearly gimmicks and have little application to nature photography. Of real importance are those which help the photographer record more succinctly or realistically the inherent nature of the subject matter. The ones most useful in colour photography are discussed below:

- A POLARIZING FILTER reduces or eliminates reflective glare from non-metallic substances like water, leaves and grass. This usually produces colours that are more intense but unchanged in hue. It will also darken blue skies, especially those photographed at right angles to the sun. (60) A polarizing filter is adjustable, and allows the photographer to control the amount of reflection by observing the scene through the lens. If the scene is to be illuminated by electronic flash, the filter's indicator mark should be turned toward the main light source. I use this filter more than any other kind.
- An ULTRA-VIOLET FILTER helps neutralize the effect of ultra-violet light, thus reducing the haze in long-distance shots, and the blueish cast of shadows, especially in snow scenes. Some photographers keep such a filter on the lens at all times for protection.
- A NEUTRAL DENSITY FILTER reduces the intensity of all light waves by a constant factor, usually two stops (ND 4X) or three stops (ND 8X). This allows the photographer to use slower shutter speeds, and/or larger apertures than might otherwise be possible, to achieve a special effect associated with motion or shallow depth of field. (60)
- COLOUR CORRECTION FILTERS are used to balance the light source to the film type. The nature photographer may occasionally need such a filter if he is shooting in a zoo, herbarium or aviary that has tungsten or fluorescent lighting.

Using Electronic Flash

If artificial light must be used by the photographer, electronic flash is far and away the best choice. Balanced for daylight film, its quick but intense flash does not harm plants or animals in any way, and seldom causes alarm. **(14)(15)** The brief duration of the light (usually less than 1/1000 second) will freeze all but the fastest action, or permit the photographer to hand-hold even long telephoto lenses without fear of camera shake.

Most electronic flashes on the market provide automatic exposure control. However, this feature is designed expressly for use indoors and will not perform reliably in the special field situations normally encountered by the nature photographer, unless he is lucky enough to own a camera with through-the-lens flash metering. Fortunately, most automatic units may also be controlled manually. If available, the small, exclusively manual (and least expensive) flash units are most suited to natural history work.

When a flash is used manually, the photographer can refer to the flash's calculator dial to determine exposure. These calculations are derived from the basic equation: Aperture = Guide Number ÷ Flash-to-Subject Distance. Bear in mind that the guide number of a flash depends on the ASA speed of the film in use. To determine the guide number, first set the correct ASA speed on the flash dial, then simply calculate the product of any pair of aperture and distance numbers. For example, if the distance is ten metres and the aperture f4, then the guide number is forty in metres. (Remember not to mix metric measure with English measure when working with flash.)

Once the guide number is established, the photographer can easily calculate the aperture necessary for correct exposure. Except in special cases, the shutter speed is set at the camera's flash synchronization speed (usually 1/60 second) and is not a factor in controlling exposure. The intensity of the light can be controlled by changing either the flash-to-subject distance or the lens aperture, whichever is more suitable.

Fill-in Flash

Fill-in flash is a simple but professional technique used to control subject contrast by throwing more light into shadow areas, and less frequently to produce sparkle in the eyes of animate subjects. **(6)** It is used almost exclusively in situations where the subject is strongly lit from the back or overhead. The aim is to record the effect of both light sources on the film without losing the dominance of the natural illumination. **(8)**

Brilliant Tones and Rich Hues

16/Summer Mustard Field
A flat, prairie field profusely spread with brilliant, yellow blooms was an irresistible opportunity. Stationing myself at one end of the tract behind a tripod-mounted, 500-mm lens, I began to scan the field, adjusting the framing and focusing until I achieved a composition that conveyed the scene's rich luminosity. The telephoto focal length made the flowers appear to be growing even more thickly. Shooting through a number of out-of-focus blossoms had the same effect as mounting a yellow filter on the lens and intensified, almost to abstraction, the yellowness of the image.

17/Leaves in a Stream
What makes the colours of this picture seem so rich? First, the lack of definition, created by the flowing water, concentrates the viewer's attention on colour and shape rather than detail. Next, and perhaps more important is the wide distribution of strong blacks and whites, which by their absence of colour, act as reference keys, accentuating the presence of any nearby colour. A 1/8-second exposure retained the coarse, frothy texture of the water's flow. A slower shutter speed would have allowed the drops and sprays to meld together, producing a creamier, calmer effect.

CHAPTER SIX

Exploring Nature at Close Range

A petrifying January morning and a chickadee perches immobile on a naked branch, a lonely puff of feathers fluffed against the cold. Clouds of condensing water vapour jetting rhythmically from each tiny nostril are transilluminated by a pale winter sun—a small drama seldom witnessed and to my knowledge never effectively recorded on film. The mechanized grace of a beetle's flight, a shrew's submarine pursuit of a shiner minnow, the prismatic sparkle of a dew-laden wildflower are all tiny pieces of nature awaiting discovery by the photographer. Capturing such intimate views requires a knowledge of close-up photography—an exacting specialty but one that is full of fascination for photographer and viewer alike.

Magnifying the Subject

Close-up photography refers to picture-taking that is done at distances less than what standard lenses normally allow. This results in film images that range from about $1/8$ the actual size of the subject to ten times life size or even greater.

In close-up work the degree of magnification directly affects a number of technical aspects such as depth of field, exposure and over-all image resolution. Varying degrees of magnification are expressed relative to life size, which is when image size equals subject size and is written one × life size. To gain a better appreciation of this amount of magnification, imagine taking a 35-mm slide frame and holding it flush to various targets—a rhino's forehead, a mosquito, a grizzly's incisor, Mount St. Helen's, a hornet's nest. In each case what lies within the frame appears as it would if photographed at one × life size.

When one is attempting to previsualize the effect of subject magnification on the image it is helpful to think in terms of the actual size of the film in use (with 35-mm cameras, film size is 24 × 36 mm), relating the subject's dimensions to this standard unit. All comparisons are linear. For a tight portrait of a chipmunk, the photographer estimates he'll need an area five times as long and wide as a single transparency, requiring a magnification of $\frac{1}{5}$ × life size. This approach is also apt for subjects requiring magnifications greater than life size, such as a housefly. In this case we see that four houseflies could be lined up comfortably nose to tail within the frame, which would call for a magnification of four × life size.

At its closest focusing distance (half a metre) the normal lens of a 35-mm SLR camera will produce a magnification about $\frac{1}{8}$ to $\frac{1}{10}$ × life size. Moderate telephotos and wide-angles are designed to produce the same degree of magnification at their respective close focusing distances, framing an area about the size of a sheet of typing paper. With the exception of mirror lenses, most extreme focal lengths do not allow this much magnification without adaptation.

Much of the subject matter of nature photography falls within a magnification range of $\frac{1}{10}$ × to $\frac{1}{2}$ × life size, which includes most reptiles, amphibians, birds, insects, wildflowers and even mammals. These subjects require the use of special close-up equipment but the actual shooting technique varies little from conventional procedures. However, at greater magnifications problems arising from poor luminosity, camera shake, inadequate depth of field, lens aberrations and exposure determination necessitate the use of more specialized approaches.

Supplementary Lenses: Close-ups the Easy Way

A supplementary lens offers an uncomplicated and inexpensive way of gaining familiarity with close-up photography. A single convex lens, it is screwed onto the prime lens like an ordinary filter and costs about the same. (43) Its magnifying power is rated in diopters and ranges from + 1 (low power) to + 10 (high power). This diopter rating is actually a measure in metres of the focal length of the supplementary lens itself. (Focal length = 1/diopter rating m.) For example, a + 2 diopter supplementary lens has a focal length of half a metre. If it is mounted on a prime lens focused at infinity, the actual focused distance becomes that of the supplementary lens (i.e. $\frac{1}{2}$ m). The photographer can work even closer to the subject simply by adjusting the focusing ring on the prime lens to a shorter distance.

The close focusing distance generated by a supplementary lens remains the same regardless of the prime lens in use. Consequently, a supplementary lens will produce greater magnification when used on a 100-mm lens than it will if used on a 50-mm lens.

Supplementary lenses may be purchased singly or in sets which usually include three lenses of + 1, + 2, and + 3 diopters. They may be mounted on the prime lens one at a time or in any combination to produce a variety of magnifications. Best results are achieved if the more powerful lenses are mounted first.

Timing, Technique and Tenacity

18/Blue-winged Teal Displaying
A drake in splendid breeding plumage, this blue-winged teal displays its primary field marks to excellent advantage, presenting a striking, decisive pose. Ordinarily, capturing such a moment on film is not easy. A number of preliminary steps are required before the photographer ever picks up a camera. First he must locate the subject. Its habitat must be one where picture-making is possible and which satisfies the photographer's artistic intentions. A way must be found to approach the animal without causing alarm—for birds it is usually by means of a blind. Once in position, the photographer should be prepared to work with the subject at length, making a number of images, perhaps on several different occasions, and hoping for that one picture which will more than justify his efforts. This solitary shot was made using a 500-mm mirror lens after I had spent only a few minutes in a stationary blind. It never hurts to be lucky.

Supplementary lenses have a number of advantages besides modest cost. Small and easy to carry, they can be attached to the lens in seconds. Unlike other close-up devices they require no special adjustments in exposure. Image quality is satisfactory at magnifications up to $1/3 \times$ life size—suitable for photographing such subjects as frogs, large butterflies or wildflowers. However, there is a price for such convenience. At magnifications greater than $1/3 \times$ life size there is a loss of sharpness at large apertures, especially around the edges of the picture. As the supplementary lenses are mounted on the lens rather than on the camera body, a number of different sets may be needed to fit lenses with different thread mount sizes.

Calculations with Supplementary Lenses

A variety of mathematical formulas are associated with close-up photography. Their derivation and theoretical application to picture-taking are interesting, but in practice many have little value in obtaining effective images. Some of the ones included here are presented in simplified versions. Easy to remember, they are those that I use frequently to double-check the accuracy of various camera settings or to anticipate equipment needs before setting out on a field trip. They are helpful but not essential, and there is certainly no need to make a formal attempt at memorization. Rather, consult this text or another when the need for such information arises.

Supplementary Lens Magnification

With the prime lens focused at infinity, magnification of supplementary lenses can be calculated by dividing the focal length of the prime lens by the focal length of the supplementary lens. As previously stated, the diopter rating of a supplementary lens is actually the inverse expression of its focal length in metres. Thus a $+3$ diopter supplementary lens has a focal length of $1/3$ m or 333 mm, and if mounted on a 50-mm lens would produce a magnification of about $1/7 \times$ life size. Suppose a photo of a chipmunk is needed at $1/5 \times$ life size using a 100-mm lens. Using the formula Focal Length of Supplementary Lens = Focal Length of Prime Lens (100 mm) ÷ Magnification ($1/5 \times$ life size), we find that a supplementary lens of 500-mm ($1/2$ m) focal length or $+2$ diopters will be needed.

Working Distances with Supplementary Lenses

When photographing wary animals, the photographer must have prior knowledge of the necessary camera-to-subject distance. With supplementary lenses this distance is synonomous with the focal length, which, we have seen, is easily derived from the diopter rating. This distance holds regardless of the focal length of the prime lens in use.

A Starting Point

The first piece of close-up apparatus to buy is a +3 diopter supplementary lens. It covers a range of useful magnifications and produces pictures of quite satisfactory quality. At only nominal cost it provides a revealing introduction to close-up photography and will probably inspire further exploration. If a more serious interest develops, the next step is to work with lens extension devices (tubes or bellows) which allow more versatility, greater magnification and better quality images.

Using Lens Extensions

These accessories are mounted between the camera body and the lens, thereby extending its close-focusing capability. Nothing more than light-tight, hollow metal cylinders, extension tubes are available in a variety of fixed lengths. Bellows operate on exactly the same principle but being constructed somewhat like an accordion, they are continuously variable throughout their range. Either device can be used with practically any lens that fits the camera. Having no optical components, lens extensions do not take away from the image quality of the prime lens.

Extension Tubes

Extension tubes may be purchased singly but they are customarily sold in sets of three, including ten, fifteen, and twenty-five-mm lengths. They can be mounted one at a time or in any combination to provide a variety of magnifications. Automatic extension tubes are designed to permit full use of the camera's operational features. Semi-automatic or manual tubes necessitate making stopped-down exposure readings and, with some cameras, manual operation of the diaphragm. Automatic tubes are well worth the small extra investment, especially if the photography of insects and other small animals appeals to you. Here the quick camera operation that automatic tubes afford is a definite advantage. (37)(59)

Extension Bellows

The amount of extension possible with a bellows is continuously adjustable throughout its range, which usually extends from fifty mm to 200 mm. Bellows are costlier and more cumbersome than extension tubes and in most situations must be mounted on a tripod. Almost all models require that through-the-lens exposure readings be made at shooting aperture. Automatic diaphragm control is usually accomplished by means of a double cable release. (15)

The close-up enthusiast who often finds himself working at magnification greater than life size will find that bellows have no equal when it comes to convenience. Should you decide to invest in a set of bellows, be sure it is equipped with a focusing rail. This essential feature permits camera, lens and bellows to be moved as a unit, allowing very fine adjustments in focusing and positioning the equipment.

Obtaining Desired Magnification with Extensions

In practice I usually decide what combination of lens and extension to use by putting them on the camera and having a look at the subject—or a similar-sized facsimile if the intended target happens to be wild and still at large. With a little experience it's not difficult to come up with a suitable combination the first time around. However, for the photographer wishing to make this determination in a more deliberate manner, the mathematical expression is quite simple: Length of Extension = Focal Length of Lens × Magnification.

From this equation it is evident that short lenses ultimately produce the greatest magnification. Indeed, at magnifications exceeding four × life size, a wide-angle is the most convenient and optically effective focal length to use.

Determining Working Distance with Extensions

This formula provides a basic guide to the working distances that will result from various combinations of lenses and extensions, an especially important consideration if one is working with nervous or wary animals. The formula is this: Working Distance = (Focal Length of Lens + Extension) ÷ Magnification. Suppose a 50-mm lens with a 25-mm extension tube is being used for insect photography. As we have seen above, this combination produces a magnification of ½ × life size. Plugging these values into the equation we see that the working distance is 150 mm, a range suitable for photographing honey bees but definitely too close for butterflies which are generally more wary.

Values derived from this equation are not precise for lenses mounted in reverse position, lenses with internal focusing, or lenses not focused at infinity. In most instances it is sufficient to remember that working distance will increase as the focal length of the lens becomes greater and the amount of extension becomes less.

Making Exposure Compensations

Extending a camera's lens for close-up photography reduces the amount of light that reaches the film. Even though the aperture is set at f4 the film may only be receiving the equivalent of an aperture of f5.6 or even smaller. If the through-the-lens meter found on most SLR cameras is used to measure the light, exposure compensation results automatically. However, if electronic flash or a hand-held light meter is used, such exposure corrections must be calculated by the photographer. Various charts, scales and formulas, including the one reproduced here, may be consulted. In practice I usually rely on a simplified formula that provides accurate exposure correction data for magnification up to two × life size. It works like this: with a 50-mm lens, compensate one stop (increase aperture size or exposure time by one setting) for every 25 mm of extension. For a 100-mm lens the required increase is one stop for every 50 mm of extension; a 200-mm lens requires an increase of one stop for every 100 mm of extension, and so on.

Reversing the Lens

At magnifications greater than life size, most standard lenses perform better if they are mounted on the extension device in reverse position. A lens-reversing ring, available at nominal cost, is all that is needed. This procedure carries the added benefit of increasing the lens-to-subject distance while maintaining the same magnification. The reversing ring may also be used to mount the lens directly on the camera, providing a degree of magnification which depends upon how much the front lens elements are recessed. When a zoom lens is reversed it acquires quite an extensive close-up focusing range. The insignificant size of a reversing ring and the weight-saving aspects of a zoom lens make this combination unbeatable for the backpacker or anyone facing strict limits on what he can carry afield.

The Macro Lens: Specially Designed for Close-ups

The convenience and high quality of a macro lens make it an indispensable piece of equipment for the close-up enthusiast. Available in focal lengths from fifty mm to 200 mm, they permit the photographer to shoot literally a caterpillar one instant and a mountain range the next. Designed to be used not only at normal distances, they are specially corrected for optimum performance at close range, most types producing a maximum magnification of $1/2$ × life size. Greater magnification is possible with extension tubes or bellows. Some zoom lenses also have built-in macro-focusing capability, offering tremendous versatility but at some sacrifice of image quality. (Fig. 3, page 77)

Close-up by Natural Light

It goes almost without saying that natural light is the ideal method of illumination for nature photography. It maintains the vital relationship between subject and environment, and in less factual images it becomes an inherent component of the picture's reality. Natural light renders rich, subtle colour and soft tones. **(38)** The feeling of naturalness and immediacy it evokes is difficult to duplicate with an artificial light source such as electronic flash. Exposure determination is simple and can be done through the lens in the normal way although stop-down readings may be necessary with some equipment. The pictorial effect of natural light can be studied thoroughly before the exposure, allowing the photographer to make purposeful adjustments to camera angle and subject placement, and to employ various types of reflectors to control subject contrast.

However, natural light does little to overcome the many technical problems of close-up photography. Generally, it is not sufficiently bright to allow the use of fine-grained colour films (ASA 64) at magnifications greater than life size. It often calls for exposure times exceeding one second due to the twin problems of diminished light transmission when lens extensions are used and the necessity for small apertures to provide adequate depth of field. In such cases the photographer must remember to compensate for reciprocity failure of the film, (discussed on page 57).

Close-up with Electronic Flash

From a technical standpoint electronic flash is the ideal illumination for any type of close-up photography. The duration of the flash (around 1/1000 second on manual firing) solves simultaneously the problems of camera shake and subject movement. The intensity of the light thrown at close range permits the use of small apertures, consequently lending much-needed flexibility to the treatment of depth of field. Its intensity and direction can be easily adjusted. Even at close range there is no heat given off that might harm delicate plants or animals, and wildlife in general pays little attention to a flash after its first firing.

At close range (less than fifteen centimetres) the harsh shadows normally associated with electronic flash are not apparent. The size of the flash reflector may often be as large as or larger than the scene being photographed and thus a softer, more even illumination results. (3) Lighting contrast can also be controlled by the use of two or more flashes as well as reflectors.

The photographer's inability to evaluate in advance the effect of the lighting is the greatest drawback of electronic flash. Skill in using flash will improve with experience but it is not possible to achieve the degree of precision and subtlety that existing light allows. Badly underexposed or even black backgrounds due to a rapid fall-off in light intensity usually characterize early attempts at using flash. (42) The artificial nature of this effect is most unsuitable for diurnal species such as bees, butterflies or small birds but it is quite fitting for the photography of nocturnal creatures. (15) The artificial appearance of pictures made in this way can be eliminated by positioning the light equidistant from both subject and background. The use of one flash usually calls for overhead placement of the flash unit. In certain situations the problem can only be overcome by using a number of flashes.

Exposure with Flash

Determining close-up flash exposure always entails an element of uncertainty due to the many variables, some often difficult to assess, that are involved in the calculations. Bracketing is a necessary precaution, and unless one is using an electronic flash specially designed for close-up work, a simple manual flash produces the most consistent results. Two special calculations are usually required. The first has already been discussed and deals with the compensations necessary for the diminished light passing through the lens due to the use of extensions. The second calculation deals with obtaining the correct aperture and flash-distance combination. Since the exposure scales of flash units do not extend into the close-up range, it is necessary to compute this information yourself using the basic formula for flash exposure: Aperture = Guide Number ÷ Flash-to-Subject Distance, (discussed on page 63). More subjective assessments must be made regarding the inherent brilliance of the subject (a white butterfly will require one stop less exposure than one of average brilliance), the effect of a flash positioned at an angle to the subject (less light will be thrown on the subject), and the combined lighting effect of two or more flashes firing simultaneously.

Electronic Flash Hardware

The smallest and least expensive manual flashes are most suitable for close-up work. Standard automatic flash units are designed to be used at normal distances only, their light sensors not being programmed for close range. A few cameras (Rolleiflex, Nikon, Olympus) are able to measure and control flash exposure automatically through the lens by taking instantaneous readings from the film plane itself; this assures accurate flash exposure regardless of the lenses or accessories mounted on the camera. Such a feature is indispensable for the specialist in close-up photography. Some companies (*e.g.* Vivitar) make automatic flashes with a special remote close-up sensor that is clipped to the front of the lens to measure light reflected from close subjects.

At high magnifications the lens-to-subject working distance is so small that normal types of illumination are unsuitable because the subject is shaded by the lens itself. The ring flash is especially designed to solve this problem. A circular electronic flash tube, it is mounted on the front of the lens to provide shadowless, frontal illumination. If some degree of lighting contrast is desired, portions of the tube may be masked to render the subject in a more three-dimensional way.

Obtaining Optimum Sharpness

The most common reason for making close-up photographs is to show the intriguing detail of the subject, to render a view that is beyond normal human vision. The following list of procedures will help you obtain optimum picture resolution:

- The most important consideration is to use a STURDY tripod or other camera support. Lock up the mirror prior to exposure to eliminate the vibration its movement causes. Weigh down the camera with a sand-filled sock. This will absorb vibrations generated by the abrupt stopping and starting of the shutter curtain. Trip the shutter with a remote release or the self timer.
- Use the best combinations of optical equipment, especially those lenses designed for close-up work. Avoid using teleconverters, high speed or zoom lenses, and supplementary lenses at high magnifications. Reverse standard lenses at magnifications greater than life size.
- Avoid extremely small or extremely large apertures.
- Use a fine-grained film and crisp lighting of average to high contrast. Electronic flash is ideal when image resolution is paramount.
- Focus with care, preferably at maximum aperture when the viewfinder is abnormally darkened by the use of lens extensions. Set up the depth of field to best advantage. Unlike that of normal distance photography, depth of field at close range is evenly distributed in front of and behind the point of focus.

Close-up Perspectives

No type of photography entails as many technical problems as that dealing with small, wild subjects in their natural habitat. Interrelated factors such as low luminosity, reduced light transmission through the optical system, inadequate depth of field and too slow shutter speeds, wind and rain and nervous subjects, all conspire to thwart the photographer's best efforts. However, such obstacles must not become an excuse for a lack of artistry, creativity or even sound technique. In the end, no one really cares how much study, hard work, patience, luck or money has been invested in a picture. The image must stand by itself and be judged in the same context as a candid, sidewalk study made with the simplest of equipment and approaches.

The specialized field of close-up photography offers the nature enthusiast another avenue of investigation, allowing him to express his fascination with a little appreciated segment of life. The techniques can be mastered in a relatively brief time and present only short-term challenge.

The real value lies in providing a vehicle to explore beyond everyday experience—not merely the world of tiny subject matter but the exciting horizons of one's own artistic and philosophical perspectives.

Figure 3
Magnification Ranges of Close-up Accessories

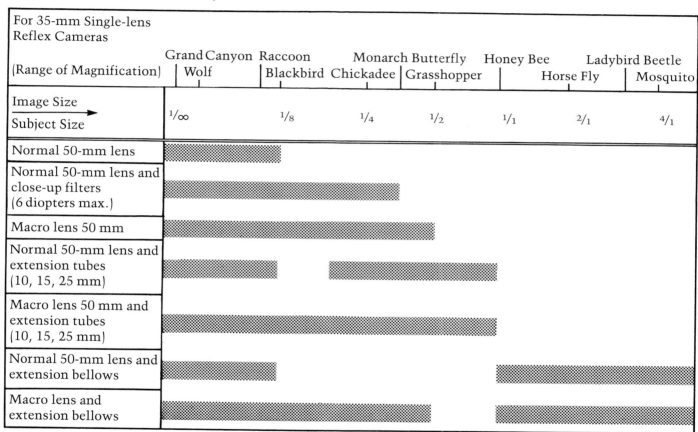

For 35-mm Single-lens Reflex Cameras (Range of Magnification)	Grand Canyon Wolf	Raccoon Blackbird	Chickadee	Monarch Butterfly Grasshopper	Honey Bee	Horse Fly	Ladybird Beetle Mosquito
Image Size → Subject Size	$1/\infty$	$1/8$	$1/4$	$1/2$	$1/1$	$2/1$	$4/1$
Normal 50-mm lens							
Normal 50-mm lens and close-up filters (6 diopters max.)							
Macro lens 50 mm							
Normal 50-mm lens and extension tubes (10, 15, 25 mm)							
Macro lens 50 mm and extension tubes (10, 15, 25 mm)							
Normal 50-mm lens and extension bellows							
Macro lens and extension bellows							

CHAPTER SEVEN

Equipment in Peril

The nature photographer's equipment is often called upon to perform under severe weather conditions. Lashing rain, frigid temperatures, blowing dust, the broiling sun—these are elements that jeopardize cameras and film. Yet such natural forces not only have a raw beauty of their own, they often lend exceptional graphic potential to an otherwise commonplace scene. A hostile environment presents special challenges and offers great rewards. If he is to succeed, the photographer must take measures to ensure that his equipment continues to function reliably when threatened by nature's destructive forces.

Generally, trouble-free operation results if equipment is kept clean at all times. After each day's outing the exterior of cameras and lenses should be wiped clean, preferably with a silicone-treated cloth or chamois. A clean toothbrush works well for sweeping out nooks and crannies, especially on the camera's deck. This simple procedure prevents dust and small particles from working into the delicate interior mechanisms.

The film chamber should be inspected on each loading and if necessary foreign matter should be removed with a blower brush. Care should be taken not to touch the shutter curtain. Optical surfaces should be kept spotless by using cleaning agents and lens tissues specially made for the purpose. (Even a clean, lint-free handkerchief may contain soap residues that will react harmfully with the chemical coatings of the lens.) It is advisable to equip each lens with a skylight or ultra-violet (UV) filter. This provides inexpensive protection to prime lens surfaces and is not detrimental to picture quality.

Water: Enemy Number One

Nothing is more damaging to pictures and film than moisture. The most commonly encountered hazard, it attacks in a variety of ways: high humidity, condensation, rain, melting snow, wet hands, perspiration, saltwater spray or full-fledged dunkings. Unfortunately, a wildlife photographer finds himself working in wet conditions more often than not as animal populations are concentrated near water bodies. Water's unique reflective properties, the photogenic quality of rain, mist or a blanket of dew, the intensified colour taken on by a wet landscape or forest all invite photographic exploration and potential equipment trouble.

Water Vapour: Unseen But Lethal

When a camera is suddenly taken into an environment of higher temperature water vapour may begin to condense on the cold metal. Water collects on exterior surfaces and delicate interior mechanisms; it not only causes corrosion and subsequent operating failure, but may also result in spotting on the film emulsion itself. A simple precaution in such situations is to make sure equipment is sealed in plastic bags until it warms up.

If one is camping, photographic equipment should be sealed in plastic bags overnight when temperatures usually drop significantly. The heavy glass and metal components cool off slowly but by dawn they are roughly the same temperature as the air. However, when the sun reappears, the air warms more quickly than the camera gear with the result that water vapour will condense on unprotected equipment.

Strange Bedfellows

If the photographer crawls out of his sleeping bag at dawn to shoot the sunrise or a passing antelope, his camera will quickly fog up and be rendered inoperable. Water vapour that condenses on the interior surface of a cold lens may delay shooting for more than an hour until the glass warms sufficiently to revaporize the moisture.

One solution is to keep the equipment (stored in plastic bags) in an open, well-ventilated spot where its temperature will not lag too far behind the ambient temperature. It is advisable, especially for large, heavy lenses, or if shooting is to commence immediately at dawn, for the photographer to place the equipment inside his own sleeping bag. Body heat will keep the glass and metal surfaces sufficiently warm to avoid moisture condensation when the photographer springs into action. If the restless sleeper finds that this practice leads to bruised shins, the equipment may be kept warm enough by placing it inside a closed styrofoam hamper along with one or two grapefruit-sized rocks that have been heated in the campfire and wrapped in towels.

Rain Protection

Care should be taken to shield the camera from rain, snow, ocean spray and other such hazards. Easy, inexpensive protection is derived from a clear, polyethylene bag. A hole should be cut in the bottom to accommodate the protruding front edge of the lens. The rest of the bag protects camera and lens, while access to camera controls is through the open end of the bag. The various dials can be read easily through the plastic and a rubber band or two holds the bag securely in place.

Of course there are a variety of foul-weather housings sold commercially. These range in sophistication from a glorified plastic bag to fully submersible plexiglass housings that allow full adjustment of all controls.

An over-sized raincoat or poncho is often suitable protection for both photographer and equipment. An umbrella affixed to the tripod itself is even more efficient and practical. (It is worthwhile to attach a permanent mounting bracket to the tripod.) This contrivance safeguards the equipment and allows the photographer to work unencumbered and somewhat out of the weather. Also, in close-up work falling raindrops are kept from jarring the subject. In the latter case a clear or white umbrella should be used.

Saltwater Hazards

Photographers working near the ocean must be continually on guard against fumbling a camera or lens, touching equipment with wet hands or allowing a stray splash or spray of saltwater to contact the equipment. Despite such caution, cameras and lenses commonly used on the coast may need servicing once or more times a year for removal of corrosion and relubrication. Even tiny, unseen droplets blown in from the sea cause unavoidable damage. One year while I was photographing coastal wildlife one of my cameras seized up on three separate occasions due to saltwater corrosion, requiring servicing each time.

Dunking a Camera

Should a camera or lens actually fall into freshwater, the best procedure is to remove the film and keep the camera immersed in water in a sealed plastic bag until it can be disassembled and dried out by a repairman. These steps minimize any short-term oxidation of metal components.

If a service facility is too remote or it is necessary that the camera continue to be used, open the camera back, remove the lens and, if possible, the bottom cover plate. Dry out the machine using any available means, but being careful not to apply excessive heat. If the camera has a metal shutter, activate it at various speeds throughout the drying process. With luck the camera may continue to function satisfactorily for a few days until it can be cleaned and relubricated.

However, should such complex equipment receive a saltwater dunking, there is little chance that it can be repaired and it is almost always more economical to replace it.

Cold Weather Precautions

A major problem when one is photographing in frigid environments is battery failure. Power supplied to a light meter, auto-exposure camera, electronic flash unit, power winder or motor drive diminishes quickly in sub-zero temperatures. When not in use such equipment should be carried beneath outer garments in warm pockets close to the body. Spare batteries should be carried and kept warm in a similar way.

The cadmium-sulfide type (CDS) of exposure meter installed in many cameras suffers great power drain when measuring the brilliant light of snowy settings. Light readings should be taken quickly and the meter should be switched off when not in use. Although less sensitive than CDS exposure meters, a hand-held selenium-cell meter is quite suitable for general purposes. Its great advantage is that it works without batteries and therefore is excellent and inexpensive insurance against failure of the camera's through-the-lens light meter.

In extreme cold, film becomes brittle and may crack if it is wound through the camera too quickly. When humidity is low, fast winding may also cause static electricity to build up as the film moves across the felt strips that prevent light from entering the cassette. This may cause sparking inside the camera which leaves branch-like markings on the film emulsion.

Low temperatures may sometimes cause the camera's shutter to slow down, causing over-exposure. This may happen when the rubberized-cloth shutters become too stiff with cold to move freely over the rollers. The lubricants of cameras manufactured before 1970 may not contain silicones and will thicken in low temperatures, causing the slow-down of shutters and other moving parts. Equipment susceptible to such cold-weather maladies is best left at home.

Wear Cotton Gloves

At sub-zero temperatures operating metal equipment with bare hands is very uncomfortable, yet winter gloves or mittens are too cumbersome to make fine camera adjustments quickly. Thin cotton gloves worn beneath the outer pair will keep the hands warm and nimble when the heavier gloves are removed. The cotton gloves serve another important function as well. When one is working behind the camera it is impossible to avoid breathing on the viewfinder occasionally. On cold days this will cause the eyepiece to fog up or even ice over. Furthermore, after a few seconds of viewing, even moist air from the eyeball will cloud up the screen. Cotton-clothed fingertips are just the thing to keep the viewfinder wiped clear and the film rolling.

Precautions for Hot Weather

Excessive heat can very quickly render a camera inoperable. A temperature of 35° C makes for a great day at the beach but if the sun is shining, the black, heat-absorbing body of a camera can soar to temperatures over 50°. Equipment damage is possible at even 45°. Lubricants become so thin that they run and gum up delicate mechanisms, and the leaves of the lens diaphragm are especially vulnerable. The balsam cement that binds the glass elements of the lens may soften, permitting the elements to separate. At over 50° bubbles may form within the glass itself, requiring expensive repairs. During the summer such temperatures are often surpassed in a glove compartment, car trunk or any tightly closed vehicle parked in the sun.

To avoid these problems equipment should be kept encased and in the shade as much as possible. As glass and metal expand at different rates, heavy telephoto lenses are prone to jamming when the temperature rises rapidly. They should be wrapped with white tape to reflect the sun's direct rays. In extreme situations equipment can be maintained at a safe temperature all day if it is kept in a closed styrofoam hamper containing a bag of ice or a commercial coolant. If these are not available, keep the hamper covered with a wet towel.

Emergencies in the Field

It is a good idea to carry a kit of small jewellers' screwdrivers to make simple, on-the-spot repairs in the field. However, the best insurance against camera failure is a second camera body. This needn't be a deluxe model or even a new one, simply an inexpensive back-up that uses the same lenses as the main camera. More than one bitter experience with a broken tripod head (even one of reputed high quality) have taught me to carry a small, emergency ball-and-socket head whenever I venture afield for more than a day.

All-risk Insurance

Every nature photographer should have all-risk insurance coverage of his equipment. This insurance can normally be bought as a simple rider on the household policy. It is quite inexpensive considering the enjoyment afforded the photographer. It allows him to work in hazardous situations from which he might otherwise be deterred for fear of equipment loss or damage. Once insured, he can hoist cameras to a treetop bird blind or shoot moose from an unsteady canoe without anxiety.

CHAPTER EIGHT

Designing Nature Photographs

Both nature and art intrigue the mind and delight the senses. As we move uncertainly into the Space Age, goaded by a persistent ethic of material- ism, and harried simultaneously by the insidious problem of over- population and the real threat of nuclear self-destruction, this enduring, comforting fact is often unfortunately forgotten. It is left to the photogra- pher, as it is to other artists, to bring sensitive reflections of nature into the workaday world.

For those without time or opportunity for observing such things, the photographer reveals the billowing grace of a gull's flight, the enchant- ment of an alpine meadow, or the bellowed roar of an elephant seal. The nature photographer's vision focuses on the realities of the external world. Looking outward with wonder, he feels compelled to communicate his experience.

Of the millions of nature photographs made each year, most have at least a small measure of artistic intent. They are meant to express a spe- cial feeling or insight that the photographer has experienced. For this to be done clearly and forcefully, considerable skill is required. The photogra- pher must know how to use his tools and materials. He also needs a practi- cal understanding of the methods of picture design, or composition. The mastery of these two components of the photographic process is prerequi- site to making images that have validity as art.

The magic that transforms a photograph into art cannot be practised or learned. Ultimately it is a product of the photographer's own genius as an individual, a reflection of his own personality. Where and how he chooses to point the camera are coloured by his particular experiences and genetic make-up. Every aspiring photographer should understand that the way he sees a winter forest or a bighorn lamb is absolutely unique and therefore of potential artistic value.

Expression through Composition

Composition is how one chooses to arrange the various parts of a picture. Its basic principles are no more difficult to learn than those of making an accurate exposure or developing a roll of film. Together with sound technical skill, the ability to design pictures confidently will allow the photographer's personal vision and philosophy to become apparent.

Composing a picture is by nature a very subjective activity. The process is most satisfying if the photographer relies on his own artistic and creative instincts. For this reason my discussion will offer a basic explanation of how composition works, leaving it to the individual to practise it, from the outset, in his own way.

Basic Strategy: The Central Theme

Composition may be thought of as a framework on which the photographer hangs his message. As such, it should state his ideas or insights clearly and directly. Before this communicating process can begin, the photographer must define in his own mind what it is he wants to say. Confronted by a natural scene, he must decide what is important and what is unimportant, the goal being to establish a central theme for the image. The choosing of a theme for the picture will guide him through all the subsequent phases of the picture-making process including, especially, his treatment of composition.

Often the central theme of a picture, or series of pictures, may be in the photographer's mind before he even leaves the house. He may intend to capture the bleakness of a desert landscape or the carnival atmosphere of a dandelion patch, or to document the nesting behaviour of a golden eagle. This being the case, he sets out on a search for those pictorial elements which will express his theme.

Alternatively, the photographer will unexpectedly come across situations in the field which excite his imagination. Before proceeding with photography he should try to analyse the reason for his initial attraction, bringing into thematic focus the scene's essential, compelling qualities. More often than not, the appeal of the scene will be primarily visual, but due to what? Is it the colour, the texture, an interesting shape, or perhaps the graphic relationships of these various parts? Once this is established the photographer can bring into play his knowledge of photographic composition to ensure a successful translation of his initial delight.

Not every worthwhile picture need contain a message or an underlying meaning. An image with strictly visual appeal is inherently valuable, pure in its artistic intention and no less valid than one which attempts to make a more readily verbalized statement. Usually it is not easy to separate the

A Decisive Moment

19/Bull Moose in a Snowsquall
"Photography is the simultaneous recognition in a fraction of a second of the significance of an event as well as of a precise organization of forms which give that event its proper expression." *
Credit for this statement goes to famed photographer Henri Cartier-Bresson. His subjects were ordinary people—living, moving, ever restless. His pictures showed how to capture for all time that fleeting instant that, more than any

other, communicates an emotion or an idea. A nature photographer should be no less demanding of his own approach to subject matter. A spring snowfall, bright inquisitive eyes, and what appears to be a disarming smile are the elements which carry this straightforward portrait of a moose beyond the ordinary. Staying low and moving cautiously, I was able to spend most of a morning with this subject: cold, wet, exciting hours of mostly watching, waiting and carefully manoeuvring for the best camera angle. The picture was made with a tripod-mounted, 500-mm lens, f4.5 at 1/250 second.

*Henri Cartier-Bresson, quoted in *The Art of Photography* (Alexandria, VA: Time-Life Books, 1971) p. 21.

visual, emotional and intellectual appeals of an image. Although we may delight in the warm hues of an autumn woodlot, is it because of the pleasant sensation the light waves impart to the brain via the retina and optic nerve or because it reminds us of a place where we grew up? In any case, we should remember that many pictures have no verbal counterpart and that photography achieves its unique status by being able to communicate ideas and feelings difficult or impossible to express in words.

Looking into the viewfinder, the nature photographer is usually confronted with a scene that is crammed with diverse and conflicting elements. It is his job to reshape this confusion into a simple plan—his composition. Without a central theme to guide his efforts, the procedure is haphazard at best. Unlike the painter who adds the necessary shapes and colours to his canvas, the photographer's task is usually one of elimination. Nothing should remain within the frame that does not in some way enhance the picture's theme. In this respect the photographer should not compromise simply because a camera was used rather than a paintbrush.

Listed below are the normal concerns which must be addressed in order to subdue or eliminate elements which detract from the central theme, as well as enhance those which promote it. The first two items are of greatest importance.

- subject matter
- the moment of exposure
- camera angle
- camera-to-subject distance
- focusing distance
- lens focal length
- depth of field (aperture size)
- shutter speed in controlling motion
- lighting
- the degree of exposure

When considered separately, most of these items are essentially camera-handling techniques. The photographer must be familiar with the operation and effect of each if he hopes to use them to full advantage in the immediate and often trying conditions of the field. More important is the necessity to realize the countless ways in which these factors may relate to each other in the process of photographic expression.

A Visual Centre of Interest

In many cases the central theme of a photograph is the result of a number of picture elements acting on the viewer's senses with more or less equal force. The success of a theme "tranquillity of a winter evening" might be due to the combined effect of pastel colours and a horizontal flow of lines and soft shapes. Some themes find expression in provocative patterns, or in the dynamic arrangement of similar figures—a cluster of wildflowers or a flight of snow geese. (2) However, most photographic compositions have, and benefit from having, a visual centre of interest: that is, one picture element which, in a graphic sense, dominates the composition. For an animal portrait, it may be the head and eyes; (36) for a landscape, a particular grove of trees; in a wildflower study, it is often the pistil and stamens. (59) The centre of visual interest anchors the design, and determines the placement of other elements within the frame. Because it is the most attractive aspect of the picture, it is usually the major vehicle of expression for the central theme.

Location of the Centre of Interest

The location of the centre of interest within the picture frame can only be effectively determined in the context of all other compositional factors.

The most important part, the prime real estate, if you will, of any picture area is its very centre. This is where the eye is likely to enter the picture and where it tends to remain, and to return unless lured away by pictorial elements elsewhere. To place the most attractive visual element in the dead centre of the frame creates a static design—an effect the photographer may sometimes find desirable. However, the eye is most attracted to movement, activity and excitement. To impart a flow and dynamism to the image it is almost always necessary to locate the centre of interest away from the middle of the picture area. (13)(26)(30) This breaks the visual inertia, setting up a graphic tension that leads the eye through the picture space in an interesting fashion.

Still, one cannot assume that placing the centre of interest on the extreme edge of the picture area will always result in a dynamic composition. It may upset the balance of the design, causing confusion or, relegated to such an uninteresting location, the centre of interest may simply lose its visual supremacy in favour of another element with a more central location. A weak centre of interest (one that has much competition from other picture elements) should be kept nearer to the central picture area than a strong one. As usual, the photographer's discretion in such matters will be a measure of his artistic judgement.

Keep it Simple

Generally speaking, a visually simple picture is more effective than a complex one. The photographer should strive for an arrangement of picture elements that, to the viewer, is evident and direct. The over-all effect should be simple but not boring, interesting but not confusing. (13) A basic prescript, especially for beginning photographers, this approach to composition induces artistic control without restricting or interfering with creativity.

1

Recording
a Sequence
of Events

20/Great Blue Heron Fishing
Nature is in a state of constant change and presents many opportunities for the photographer to record a series of events. To be effective, the pictures in the sequence must show obvious common elements that will meld them into a strong unit and focus attention on the development of change in the series as a whole. The sequence will be more telling when the rate of change appears to be constant. If picture #1 differs from picture #2 by amount X, picture #3 should differ from picture #2 by the same amount X, and so on. In this way, maximum continuity and coherence will be achieved. In the heron sequence, *the same framing was maintained throughout, and in each picture the shutter was released at the apex or finishing point of the heron's movement. Fortunately, the water was mirror smooth during the action, creating a momentary record of the passing events. Notice how the spreading ripples in the third photograph create a necessary contrast between this and the first picture.*

2

3

Picture Elements: the Ingredients of a Composition

Shape, line, texture, and colour are the basic picture elements of any composition. These are the raw materials, the ingredients of the image. In developing compositional skill the photographer needs to become accustomed to removing the labels from his subject matter. In this way it is easier to make an objective analysis based on the subject's visual appeal. A clump of grass is seen as a series of vertical lines, a badger in terms of shape and texture, a butterfly's wing as a multi-coloured triangle. The photographer moulds these ingredients into an effective design.

Shapes: the Building Blocks of Design

Shape is the essential ingredient in most photographs. Shapes appear in nature in infinite variety. A typical ramble through the woods will bring many shapes to the photographer's attention. Some may be perceived as variations on three basic geometric figures. There are circles—mushrooms, a dew drop, blueberries, woodpecker holes, the sun; triangles—spruce trees, rose thorns, flower petals, mountains; (22) and rectangles—tree trunks, the segments of a spider's web, a cliff face. (61) Other natural shapes are more complex, being freeform combinations of geometric figures which have lost their formal identity.

Whenever a shape is placed within the picture frame, there will also be generated a negative shape—that part of the picture area lying outside the positive shape, usually referred to as the background. Whenever the positive shape changes in substance or position, the negative, or background shape, will also be altered. (24) The nature photographer's awareness of this relationship is important, especially in pictures where an ecological or environmental motif may be expressed in terms of the picture's setting.

The ability to isolate and define shape in the visual world brings to the photographer's attention many interesting images that he might otherwise have passed without noticing. Once developed, this awareness is a precious gift, enabling the photographer to see beyond the superficial.

Lines: Compositional Mortar

Strictly speaking, a line has only one dimension, and therefore no visual actuality. It merely occupies a position, setting the limits of a shape or space. In a graphic context, lines are long, thin picture elements: a strand of hair, a tree branch, the veins of a leaf, the halo-outline of a backlit grizzly bear, the stem of a daisy, the horizon. (2)

In some photographs, lines have a visual power and presence of their own and may comprise the primary thrust of the composition. For most pictures, however, lines are used to support and organize other visual elements. They may be used to join one part of a picture to another, lead the eye through the picture in a purposeful manner, balance the design, or divide the picture space to effect variety.

Lines can be thick, thin, dotted, dashed, rippled, curved, jagged, wavy, feathery, scratchy—the possibilities are endless. There can even be a sensation of line where none exists. This occurs when a finger, a heron's beak, the stare of a lynx or the forward sweep of a jackrabbit's ears directs attention to a specific feature in the distance.

As a result of our experiences and traditions, certain types of lines are associated with certain feelings. Vertical lines suggest life, dignity, power and resistance to change. (61) Horizontals represent quiet and repose, the calm of the sea, death, the earth and sky. (54) Danger, motion, action and emotion find expression in diagonal lines. (22) Circular or curved lines signify grace, growth, passivity and frequently eroticism. (29) Like any graphic symbol, a particular type of line may not always evoke the same reaction. Nevertheless, in appropriate circumstances, their representational value can often help strengthen the theme of a picture.

By developing an awareness of naturally occurring lines and a knowledge of their effect and use in picture design, the photographer can begin to compose pictures with greater assurance of achieving the intended effect.

Visual Texture: Multi-sensory Appeal

Rough, shiny, silky, bumpy, bristly, slippery, grainy, wrinkled, hard or spongy—the list of textures is limited only by the variety of physical matter. (4)(47) Texture is essentially a tactile quality. Through day-to-day experience we develop a strong association between seeing and touching. Eventually this culminates in a visual appreciation of surface texture sufficient to transmit a stimulus to the brain that achieves an effect almost as real as the actual touching.

Any image gains strength when it appeals to senses other than the visual, and of all our physical senses, touch is most readily communicated by visual means. Hence, it can be usefully incorporated into the photographic process.

All textures are manifested visually by the interplay of light and shadow, which defines the surface material. The direction and quality of the lighting are the instruments which the photographer uses to express and control texture. (8)(9)

As with the picture elements previously discussed, the photographer needs to become "sensitized" to the wealth of textures that exist in nature. There are fuzzy muzzles, silken sand dunes, polished leaves, and hard, rumpled backs of alligators. Besides such actual physical textures, the photographer should also be alert for those not directly associated with the sense of touch due to the large size of their unit mass. Viewed from a

Framing the Essence of a Scene

21/Cormorants in the Fog
Frequently a scenic picture owes its success as much to what the photographer chooses to exclude as to what he has actually recorded. The mysterious, almost ominous, aura of this photograph is produced, in part, by the implication that the fog stretches endlessly. With a telephoto lens, I was able to sustain the mystic quality by excluding foreground elements, which were quite distinct, and peripheral areas where the mist was beginning to dissipate. The long lens also helped to intensify the effect of the fog. The seabirds seem suspended in a haze, emphasizing the surreal aspects of the image.

22/Above the Clouds

Unlike the photograph of the cormorants, this landscape is organized on traditional compositional principles. The cloud banks trace a classic "S" curve, weaving their course around the hills in a sensual, rhythmic manner. In contrast to their soft, sinuous aspect, the trees provide upthrust, rapier-like, geometric shapes and the mountainsides angle sharply through the scene. Each force counteracts and heightens the effect of the other, beckoning the eye to play alternately over the differing textures, and to follow the strong diagonal lines and patterns throughout the photograph. Again, I used a telephoto lens to isolate the graphic interplay of these natural elements.

distance, texture springs from such phenomena as a tightly knit caribou herd, a field of wildflowers, a thickly forested mountainside, or a cloud bank. (22)

Colour's Pervasive Influence

Along with shape, colour is the photographer's most expressive instrument. It helps distinguish and identify other picture elements, communicates mood and emotion, and in many pictures is a visual delight all of itself. (62) To use colour effectively the photographer should learn to see it in terms of film and camera, and develop an awareness of the way it attains its appeal.

Strong Colour

Strong colours are pure and saturated. They are undiluted by grey, black or white. They achieve the greatest effect when lit directly by flat, strong sunlight. The basic hues—blue, green, yellow, and especially red, produce the most visual attraction. So powerful is their effect that they easily dominate other picture elements, an important consideration, especially when they are likely to conflict with the composition's centre of interest. (1)

Strong colours readily express emotion. Red and yellow are considered to be warm hues. They convey vitality, gaiety, boldness and strength. (57) In contrast, the coolness of blue and green is evocative of serenity, calmness and passivity. (61) Any colour, regardless of hue, gains visual strength when set off against the neutral tones of black, white or grey. (17)

When many strong colours are found in the same composition, a struggle for viewer attention is created. The gaudy, carnival-like impression this creates is suitable to some themes. However, without careful control, it can cause confusion, throwing the composition off balance and disrupting the unity of the theme. A photograph incorporating a limited range of saturated hues and areas of neutral contrast (grey, black, white) will retain a strong impact and at the same time be explicit in its statement. The visual volatility of these colours is most readily expressed and controlled by simple, direct designs.

Muted Colour

Expressive of a variety of feelings, muted colours readily adopt the mood or atmosphere suggested by the lines and shapes of a composition. Colours become muted by the addition of grey, black or white. In the photographic image this may result from the inherent structure of the subject matter, the lighting conditions or the way in which the film is exposed and developed. Shadows and under-exposure degrade the purity of the hue. Reflections, flare, atmospheric scattering of light and over-exposure desaturate the colour by the introduction of white. (21)

The photographer can mute colour in a number of ways. He can shoot through grass, foliage or branches located near the camera in the picture's foreground. (16) Rendered on film as out-of-focus blurs, such elements cause light waves to become scattered and diffused, desaturating the colours of the image. For the same reasons working in rain, smog, snow, mist or fog will also result in softer hues. (22) Colour will be diluted by using soft-focus lenses or filters, fogging the lens surface with breath, or defocusing. In a similar way the colour of moving subjects will be desaturated if a slow shutter speed is used to cause blurring. (35)(29) Another technique is to induce lens flare by angling the camera so that light rays direct from a specular source (clear sun or electronic flash) strike the film. In these instances the effect should be judged at shooting aperture.

Colour Harmony
Colour harmony results when a single hue dominates the composition. The harmony may be restrained as in the case of a combination of forest green, lime green and olive green, or more exuberant and wide ranging as would result from a blue, green, and turquoise scheme. (2)(61) Even strongly contrasting colours such as blue and red may be harmoniously linked by using an intermediate hue such as purple. Harmony is more easily attained with muted colours than with strong ones. Sometimes a harmonious colour scheme can be accentuated by including a small area of a contrasting hue. (30)

A picture design that is based on colour harmony automatically achieves a coherent visual effect. Usually it is suited to images with calm, peaceful themes and those with compositions incorporating horizontal lines, symmetrical shapes and repeated patterns. (39) The rhythms that are naturally generated by harmonious colour schemes create great visual pleasure simply on their own merit. In nature, colour harmony is always prevalent: the earthy oranges, rusty browns and faded reds of autumn; the fresh range of greens in a forest glade; the splotches of brown, tan and charcoal in a musk ox's shaggy coat.

Colour Contrast
Colours that are opposite or nearly opposite (red/green, orange/blue, yellow/purple, light/dark, warm/cool) interact strongly when used in the same composition. (23)(62)(13) The eye will bounce back and forth between the contrasting hues—the more saturated the colour, the greater the effect. To test this for yourself colour a small, solid circle of red or orange onto a sheet of blank, white paper. Stare at the circle for about thirty seconds and then turn the paper over. Immediately a blue circle will appear on the paper—the brain's way of bringing the eye's colour sensitivity back into balance. Under normal conditions, the eye automatically

Special Effects in Black and White

23/Trumpeter Swans on Goldstream River Delta
Learning to see photographically is essential to producing consistently strong images. What looks quite impressive to a human may look very commonplace to a Nikon, and vice versa. At first glance this scene appeared lacklustre—a washed-out, colourless expanse of brown and grey—but I did notice that bright reflections on the water's surface created a situation of great lighting contrast. By choosing settings that would render the highlight areas correctly (the swans and sandbars) yet so under-expose the remainder of the scene that it would appear black, I achieved strong pictorial elements that could be worked into an appealing design. Under-exposing $2^{1}/_{2}$ stops from the meter reading, I framed the scene (shot downward from a mountain ridge) so that the swans and sandbars formed a subtle but effective counterbalance of rhythms.

24/Bonaparte's Gull Preening

The dawn sun illuminates this preening gull, but it is not yet high enough to light up the gravel bar that the bird is standing on or impart colour to the water. The high-contrast lighting of this scene was exploited in the same way as the preceding one. Under-exposed by two or three stops, the film still accurately records the brightest whites of the bird and at the same time affords a variety of grey tones ranging all the way to black. Slivers of light playing on the water serve to balance the composition, while the touch of red in the leg accentuates the absence of colour.

prevents over-stimulation of a certain colour by intermittently seeking out a contrasting hue. This perceptual characteristic can be used to create visually exciting compositions in which the eye moves continually about the picture.

Colour contrast is a powerful design tool, and must be handled carefully by the photographer. The warm colour component is generally the most striking, while the opposing cool hues recede. Obviously, it may be difficult to use colour contrast when the visual centre of interest happens to be the weak-hued partner. In such situations the centre of interest must dominate in other ways—greater size, more interesting shape, more advantageous placement. Its primacy may even be strengthened if it is isolated within an expanse of the opposing colour—a blue jay photographed against a blurred background of an autumn forest for example.

Striking patterns and rhythms can also be built with contrasting colours. Because of the considerable impact of the colour relationship, simple designs usually work best. More complex arrangements may easily become confused and discordant. In the autumn, a mixed coniferous/ deciduous woodland is just one of the many opportunities to work with the contrasting colour patterns that nature offers.

Principles of Design: Arranging the Raw Ingredients

Shape, line, colour, texture—these constitute the basic "stuff" of which a picture is made. How they may be arranged within the picture frame is ultimately the most enjoyable part of photography. There is of course no "correct" way to arrange the pictorial elements that have just been described. Even with only a few elements it is impossible to exhaust the design possibilities. However, some compositions obviously work better than others. The photographer will find his pictures come together in an effective way when he has a clear idea at the outset of what he wants to communicate in the image. Most of the time, the nature photographer is interested primarily in emphasizing his subject matter and seeks to build a composition that will present it to best advantage.

Just realizing the graphic significance of the subject matter is a major step toward good composition. Having become "sensitized" to the lines, shapes, colours and textures of the natural world, the photographer can turn his attention to arranging these elements into a design which will promote the central theme.

This process may be carried out in a natural, intuitive way, the photographer developing a composition that feels good to him. Alternatively, the design may be worked out in an analytical manner, wherein the photographer rationally determines the arrangement of elements in accordance with formal design principles. In practice, most photographers use a combination of these two extremes.

Although we people communicate primarily through the spoken or written word, photography communicates visually. For this reason, it often expresses ideas that can only be appreciated by the eye: ideas that do not translate into words. Designing a photographic image is a multi-dimensional undertaking. So many factors—emotional, visual, intellectual, philosophical—come into play that it is impossible to definitively describe or explain the process. That is, of course, a large part of photography's challenge, intrigue and magic.

Principles of design are reference points, working together to help the photographer in the same way a compass guides the traveller. They do not say turn right or left, go faster or slower, retrace a route or stop for a picnic. They merely point to the north, and it is left to the photographer, as it should be, to choose where and how to conduct his exploration.

Dominance

All design is based on the principle that some visual elements are more attractive than others. More than any other factor, this determines the eventual outcome of a composition. The photographer's central theme will prevail only if it finds expression in the dominant pictorial elements. Of course this may be accomplished in many ways, from relying on a single, striking element that carries the full thrust of the theme, to using the combined effect of a number of elements working in a unified manner.

Weighing the appeal of picture elements is not a cut-and-dried matter. Much depends on the over-all context of the image and, ultimately, the perceptions of the viewer. With this in mind the photographer proceeds, basing his judgements on visual psychology which espouses the following kinds of conclusions:

- Red is more attractive than yellow.
- A large shape will draw more attention than a small one.
- Rough textures are more striking than smooth ones.
- Difference is more alluring than conformity.
- Curved lines are more intriguing than straight lines.
- Jagged lines are more exciting than curved ones.
- Diagonal movement draws more attention than either vertical or horizontal movement.
- Light is more attractive than dark.
- Sharpness is more striking than blur.

Taken out of context, all these relationships are probably true. However, what is more attractive: a curved red line or a jagged yellow one? A grey, diagonal, rough texture or one that is smooth, vertical and turquoise? These simple examples give an idea why dealing with composition is so subjective and challenging. Consciously or unconsciously, the photographer makes such decisions every time he looks into the viewfinder.

Exploring a Special Habitat

25/Wild Shoreline
A good way to get started in nature photography is to concentrate on a specific habitat. It could be a stretch of local coastline, an alpine meadow, a marsh, a city park or even the backyard—any convenient place for which the photographer feels a special affinity. Visiting the chosen site regularly, he may attempt to document the spectrum of life, ranging from the decomposers to the predators at the apex of the food chain. He may wish to log the yearly cycle of seasonal change, describe the relationships among species of plants and animals, or record the effects of atmosphere, precipitation or dessication. On an interpretive level he may explore the patterns of light and shadow, or express himself by the artistic rendering of natural forms, structures and designs. This picture and the one of the kingfisher are the results of this approach; they are among thousands I have made in an ongoing exploration of a single coastal habitat.

26/A Kingfisher Snag

Buffeted by frequent gales, pounded by surf and waves, the outer coast of Vancouver Island is rugged, isolated and largely uninhabited. It is one of my favourite places. All life there seems in some way affected by the sea's influence. A kingfisher, backlit by a setting sun, hunts a tidal pool from a snag tossed ashore by a storm. On a symbolic and personal level, the picture brings together the basic forces of life— sunlight, air, water, plants, animals, predation—all appropriately couched in an aura of mystery.

Contrast and Harmony

Contrast and harmony are complementary principles, evident to one degree or another in almost every photograph. Contrast is used to direct attention to a specific picture element by showing how it differs from other elements or aspects of the composition. The blur of a bounding jack-rabbit against a sharp, grassy background, a wobbly moose calf amidst its mother's powerful legs, a yellow avalanche lily set against a blue sky, an alligator's ridged back in a glass-smooth pool—the comparisons may be based on graphic elements such as line, shape, colour and texture, or on more abstract relationships such as frailty and strength or growth and decay. (60) When using contrast, the photographer should make clear whether the contrasting principle itself is the central theme of his picture, or if he is just using it to bring more attention to the main subject. The former approach requires that each aspect of the relationship receive equal emphasis, (27) whereas in the latter the dominance of the main subject must be maintained. (37)(35)

Harmony brings emphasis to the central theme of a photograph by repeating its important aspects. For example, a herd of bulky, hump-postured buffalo may be mirrored by a similar formation of hills or mountains in the background, creating a harmony of shapes. Harmony may be generated by repetitions of line, texture, and colour as well. (2) However, it also results when a particular quality or mood is repeated using a variety of picture elements. (50) A feeling of serenity may be expressed by pastel colours, horizontal lines, and smooth textures. Being a repetition of similar aspects of the central theme, harmony works to diffuse the importance of the visual centre of interest, should there be one. At the same time, however, the main theme of the picture gains strength.

Balancing for Unity

A composition that is not in balance is distressing to look at. It produces the same disturbing feeling as a melody sung off key or someone walking around with a shoe untied.

Good picture balance does not mean that the visual weight of picture elements should be equally distributed on both sides of a central vertical axis. Although this is a popular notion, it has no real validity. The most obvious reason is that visual attraction has no connection with the force of gravity. Pictures can exhibit imbalance in reference to the horizontal axis just as easily as they can to the vertical. (51) Further, most successful images are, by this definition, poorly balanced, leaving the value of this approach in question.

This principle of composition concerns itself with making a balanced use of the picture area, rather than a balance of visual elements. The area that is allotted to the photographer to make his statement is a finite quantity, and a small one at that. Every square millimetre is precious. A picture is out of balance when parts of it do not help carry the photographer's message.

This does not mean that a balanced design has its picture elements spread evenly over the picture area. Empty areas, or areas passively used, are not necessarily wasted. Often, passive areas work as an effective contrast to accentuate more dynamic aspects of the composition. **(23)(24)** Many ideas—isolation, loneliness, freedom, for example—are effectively expressed by passively used picture areas. **(54)**

Specifically, one should ask if each section or area of the picture space is working for the benefit of the whole. A particular area may be doing nothing, or worse, detracting from the central theme, throwing the composition off balance, deflecting it from the intended goal. A careful border-to-border examination of the scene through the viewfinder will alert the photographer to any changes that may be required.

Rhythm

Rhythm is an essential component of many natural forces; a nature photographer, or any artist for that matter, cannot help but be affected by it. The regular passing of the seasons, the alternation of night and day, the cadence of a running antelope, the radiating petals of a daisy, the progressive sequence of a fir tree's branches, the heartbeat of a hummingbird and even our daily routines are either based on, or conditioned by, rhythm.

Rhythm arises from a repetition of accent and interval that produces a pattern. **(53)** On the simplest level it is expressed by a single accent at regular intervals, as would be evidenced in a well-made picket fence. More complex rhythms incorporate repetitions of varied sequences using a greater variety of unit parts. These patterns may be formal and unchanging; however, they become more expressive and interesting when modulated by subtle variations of the pattern. This effect is often encountered in nature: a line of parading ducklings, an expanse of walrus-packed shoreline or the rolling foothills of the Rockies being several examples. **(47)(34)** Rhythms find expression in lines, shapes, colours and textures. They can show movement through progressive changes in the components of a pattern which often produces dynamic, forceful designs not unrelated to a musical crescendo.

More than any other principle of composition, rhythm accounts for visual pleasure. The photographer should develop a sensitivity to its natural occurrence and learn how to adapt it effectively to his medium. Many rhythms encountered in the field need further defining. **(27)** Among the various technical controls at the disposal of the photographer, a change in camera angle is often all that is needed. With animate subjects, the timing of the exposure is frequently the critical factor. **(32)(33)** When the photographer's primary aim is visual pleasure, stark isolation of the rhythmic elements usually proves to be the most effective treatment.

Tuning In

To prepare myself mentally for a creative photographic session, I use a variation on an approach made popular by Minor White. It involves attaining a "sensitized mind", that is, an open, blank state of perception that is highly attuned to visual stimuli. White and his students used Zen philosophy and meditation techniques to prepare themselves for a photographic session. This approach might seem a little airy to some photographers, but there are definite merits to the underlying principles. My sensitization process is fairly simple. I walk slowly and carefully for the first while that I am in the woods. I stay on easy trails where progress is both quiet and smooth. I always go alone. I listen and look and concentrate on my surroundings. I let ideas and images flow to me, trusting evaluation to intuition. I don't want past photographic conditioning about what should look good to interfere. It might be five or ten minutes or even an hour before I feel like setting up the camera but this usually happens quite decisively.

Go Your Own Way

Of course there is much more to picture design than can be discussed in a text of this kind. The infinite variety of subject matter, situation and artistic intent inherent in the practice of nature photography belies any pat formulas of composition. These suggestions have been made especially with the novice photographer in mind, but they have value at any stage of creative photography. To summarize them briefly, the photographer should strive for a simple, unified composition, and his approach to the design of a picture should be guided by a central theme. Aside from the theories and principles associated with picture composition, the photographer must, above all, trust and believe in the validity of his own creative vision and artistic instinct.

**Focusing
for Effect**

27 / Woodland Meadow

The survival of many plant species is dependent on the visual attractiveness of the flowering parts. Simple necessity has afforded them an uncommon beauty. Without it, pollination would not take place. Despite the exquisite beauty of the subject, pictures of wildflowers grow repetitive if the photographer is content with one hastily conceived portrait after another. Although "collecting" species on film has its attractions, greater enjoyment is to be had if the photographer also expresses the plant's relationship to its environment, the geometry and pattern of its growth and development, or its emotional and symbolic value. This composition is barely under control, but the unrestrained nature of the design is expressive of the freedom and innocent vigour of a woodland meadow. The success of the image hinges on the choice of focus distance and depth of field.

CHAPTER NINE

Practising at the Zoo

No environment on earth harbours a greater variety of animals than the local zoo. New concepts in management have given rise to enclosures which attempt to simulate the animals' natural habitats. It certainly makes it easier to produce pictures that are often difficult to distinguish from ones taken in the wild. Does this mean the wildlife photographer is an endangered species? Not in the least. Exciting photos of animals, especially close-ups, can be taken at zoos or game farms. However, the most memorable pictures will continue to be gleaned from the wild.

Zoos are excellent places to learn and practise some of the techniques of wildlife photography. Animal behaviour may be observed in a semi-natural environment, allowing the photographer to gain experience in predicting activities and behaviour sequences: this in turn assists in correct timing of the instant of exposure. The photographer will discover which lenses are best suited for which types of animals. Study may be given to determining how different qualities, quantities and colours of light are used to render on film the tremendous diversity of animal texture, form and movement. New equipment may be tested under controlled conditions approximating those in the field where second chances seldom occur. By taking careful notes of such factors as how exposures were made (film, lighting, aperture and shutter speed) the photographer will quickly improve his technical competence. Records of this sort are essential for consistent results with electronic flash or close-up equipment. Thoroughness and patience at this stage will pay dividends later.

Eagle on a Leash

The basic concepts underlying photography both at the zoo and in the wild are very similar. The major problem is to control or predict the activity of the animals. In a zoo, it is accomplished by the use of bars, plate glass and concrete moats, while in the wild, instinctive behaviour patterns are used to direct the picture-making process. Photographers take advantage of the fact that animals are tied to reproductive patterns (the bird's nest, the wolf's den), food and water requirements (salt licks, bird feeders, carrion) and other vital habits (activities associated with migration flyways, dust baths, game trails) just as securely as they are retained by a cage.

Removing Bars

One of the first problems encountered at the zoo is the disturbing presence of bars and screens between the lens and the subject. In the field it could just as easily be a tree limb or blade of grass and the same procedures are used to subdue their effect or make them disappear entirely. If there are no retainers and the animals are not dangerous, the photographer will naturally push his lens through the bars, or mesh, and shoot away. When this is not possible, the lens should be rested right up against the caging. If it is mesh, try to centre the lens over one opening, using the largest aperture possible. Shoot through the area of screen that has the least highlight or glare. Dull-coloured fencing will yield the best results. If flash is being used, do not let it illuminate the portion of the screen through which the camera is shooting. Lens focal length is another important consideration. The longer the lens, the easier it is to eliminate the wires or bars due to the decrease in depth of field.

Of course, a camera with through-the-lens viewing and a depth-of-field preview mechanism will allow the photographer to see just how well he is doing and he may even choose to stop down somewhat from maximum aperture.

These procedures are usually quite effective. The only drawback may be a decrease in contrast of the final photograph, depending on the arrangement and size of the foreground elements through which the shot was made.

Shooting Through Glass

Many types of animals are retained by glass partitions. This presents a different problem: reflection. Again, the picture should be made with the lens pressed tightly against the glass. This should effectively remove all reflection. If this method does not allow satisfactory composition and the photographer is forced to step back from the glass or shoot at an angle, then it is necessary to shield the glass from easily reflected objects (hands, forehead, chrome camera bodies). A piece of black matte cardboard about thirty centimetres square usually suffices. A hole is cut in the material and the lens pushed through. This will prevent any reflections from appearing on the portion of the glass through which the camera is aimed. The farther the camera is from the glass and the shorter the focal length of the lens, the larger the shield must be. When one is shooting under exist-

Refining a Natural Design

28/Water Logs
Any natural habitat—a meadow, forest, mountainside or seashore—is filled with exciting designs. Some are strikingly obvious but uncontrolled. To be truly expressive they must be further defined by the photographer. Others may be only suggestions of design which the photographer must nurture to provide the needed form and direction. The exciting graphic potential of these stained, wizened trunks would be readily noticed by any alert photographer. At first I had trouble isolating the essence of their attraction. As I tried to find an appropriate way to frame this scene, irrelevant elements kept intruding, diluting the strength of the composition. Finally, I realized that the forceful vertical elements were the key to the scene's strength, and settled on this picture which uses the water's reflective properties and a vertical format to extend and intensify the pattern.

29/Autumn Stream Swirl

Patterns and rhythms give organization, structure and meaning to life: hence, their tremendous visual appeal. The photographer should try to develop a sensitivity to these relationships. Skill in finding visual patterns can be practised anywhere—in the shower, while driving to work or even watching television. It's not particularly difficult to do; it's just difficult to remember to do. There are a variety of distinct, interesting patterns evident in this picture, all united by their common colour elements. The natural flow of the water helps to organize this rich array of subject matter. The eye is drawn to the bull's eye configuration of the swirl, grows bored, jumps out to study the detailed bits of foam and vegetation about the periphery and then follows the symbolic and graphic flow of pattern back to the vortex. When the picture was made, the water was actually circling very slowly and I had only a rough idea of how this image would turn out. The exposure lasted about fifteen seconds.

ing light, a polarizing filter may be placed on the lens and adjusted to remove some types of reflection. If electronic flash is being used, the unit should also be placed flush with the glass to prevent its light from reflecting into the lens.

Backgrounds

Once the photographer has successfully coped with the obstacles in front of the animal, he must contend with what lies behind it. The worth of any picture depends to a great degree on the manner in which the background is handled. At the zoo, this part of the picture will usually be fraught with perils—signs, drinking troughs, pipes, brick walls, etc. Sometimes it is possible to incorporate such elements into the composition but often it is easier to subdue or eliminate them. In the wild, the background elements will of course be natural, but they will not necessarily be compatible with the design or theme of the photograph.

The most obvious remedy is to change the camera position so that the animal is shot against a more suitable background. Alternatively, the photographer may begin by choosing the background and then wait for the animal to move in front of it, a common field technique. Another way to exclude distracting elements is to use a long-focal-length lens, changing the perspective so that less background appears in the photograph. One of the most common procedures is to simply use a large aperture, thus limiting depth of field to a degree that renders the background as an unintelligible blur.

When one is using colour slide films with relatively narrow exposure latitudes, it is possible to use electronic flash so that the subject is illuminated correctly but objects farther away (i.e. backgrounds) are so underexposed as to appear black in the resulting slide. Flash is especially appropriate for animals with nocturnal habits.

In actual practice it is often necessary to combine several of these suggestions to obtain the desired results.

Lighting

The lighting in most zoos is designed for the comfort of the animals and the viewing public. It is often notoriously poor for photography. When shooting colour film, the photographer's first concern is matching the film to the colour temperature of the light source. The best procedure is to load daylight film which will also be balanced for electronic flash. As well, I carry two filters, an 80a for use with tungsten light and a magenta (fl) filter for shooting under fluorescent light. Animals kept outside are frequently shaded by buildings or trees and it is necessary to plan the shooting session for a time when the lighting is at its best.

Many outdoor cages are roofed-over, dingy affairs and available-light photography often yields poor results. In such cases electronic flash may be the most satisfactory means of illumination. It is much the same situation as one would encounter photographing at a bird nest in a dark forest. The brief duration of light allows hand-holding even the longest lenses and will stop the action of most animals, including birds in flight. The high-contrast character of electronic flash lighting may be softened by wrapping a layer of white handkerchief over the reflector. This will require an exposure compensation of about one stop. Interesting effects may be achieved by using the flash off the camera for sidelighting, toplighting, or even backlighting.

Friend Tripod

At the zoo, the low lighting conditions and unusual lethargy of the animals make long telephoto exposures a common type of shot; consequently the use of a tripod becomes necessary. Often, a telephoto lens will not focus as close as needed. An extension tube inserted between camera body and lens easily solves this problem, but the resulting increase in magnification makes a tripod even more essential. Whenever possible, regardless of shutter speed, use fences, walls, bars, etc. as a means to steady hand-held shots.

Beginnings

There are many wild and free animals that take advantage of the variety and abundance of food and plants concentrated within the zoo. Squirrels, rabbits, raccoons and all kinds of birds may be seen roaming at large. They present an excellent opportunity for a beginning photographer to take his first striking wildlife portrait. Most of these animals are accustomed to humans and will allow a closer approach than normal. They may also be baited easily to a location which has been prepared for photography.

Because animal photographs at the zoo are a technically simple accomplishment, something needs to be done to make them outstanding. It may be the lighting or a unique camera angle. A yawn, stretch, snarl, or yelp may lend dynamism to the portrait. Generally, it is important to have the animal engaged in some activity. This requires a degree of patience and the ability to anticipate. However, just as with work in the field, the amount of effort put into the photography will be readily apparent in the finished image.

Colour Harmony
in a Marsh

30/Caspian Tern Flying over Gulls
For me, colour is the most dynamic of all the elements of pictorial design. In the field the diversity of natural colour often forces the photographer to be selective. If not carefully controlled, a number of individual hues may simply work to neutralize each other, causing the picture to lose direction and emphasis. In this photograph the cool, light tints of green, blue, and grey dominate the composition. The fiery red of the tern's bill adds a necessary accent, and draws attention to the centre of interest.

31/Bittern in Cattails

The colour and pattern of a bittern's plumage provide camouflagic protection for the bird in its reedy, marsh habitat. The harmonious visual relationships that result offer exciting photographic possibilities. Working in a mobile blind one cold March morning, I was trying to stalk a common gallinule when this bittern landed noisily in the cattail stands near me. The bird soon grew alarmed but not before I was able to make several exposures. The pastel tones of the scene are accentuated by the diffused light from a partially overcast sky and by the limited depth of field which softened the stems in the background and foreground.

Adventures with Wildlife

CHAPTER ONE

Concealing the Photographer's Presence

For many people, a glimpse of a fox or deer in the wild is a memorable event; for others, the long-range identification of an elusive bird is an exciting accomplishment. However, for the wildlife photographer, such activities are usually only the preliminaries of an undertaking that must see him approach a wild creature far closer than it finds instinctively tolerable, and then apply the considerable technical and artistic skills necessary to produce a photograph of unique value.

In the first half of this century the merit of a wildlife photograph was often due to the fact that the species depicted had never or rarely been previously recorded. Thus, most wildlife pictures were of value simply for the taking. Today, few, if any, of the roughly fifteen hundred species of birds and mammals in North America have not been photographed. Of these, many have been photographed literally thousands of times by thousands of photographers. To make a fresh and significant statement about any of these life forms is an achievement of lasting satisfaction. In meeting this challenge, one of the simplest and most useful tools at the wildlife photographer's disposal is the blind.

Recollections from a Photographic Blind

Again I was awakened by the electronic hum of a mosquito foraging inside the cramped quarters of the blind. Blotting sweat from my eyes with a dangling shirttail, I peered out through the long tunnel of lens into the broiling, white heat of the Saskatchewan prairie.

The nest platform was empty. The four young marsh hawks had scattered into the relative coolness of the surrounding cattails and remained still except to snap occasionally at the blur of a passing horsefly. Like me they were waiting for the return of the hunting mother. During my two days of photography at the nest site she had airlifted over thirty mice and voles to the ravenous brood.

Unique and Fleeting Moments

32/Oystercatchers on Parade
Almost all species of North American vertebrates have been photographed, many of them tens of thousands of times. I became pretty discouraged when I first realized this, feeling cheated that no one had saved anything for me to take pictures of. Then it suddenly dawned that this state of affairs left me free to pursue my subjects any way I wanted. Someone else had been charged with the mundane task of making the innumerable "record" shots, the photographs needed to say simply that this animal exists, that it has four legs and a tail, that it will be henceforth filed under "carnivora". *Whew! Talk about a lucky break. The pressure is off. We can be as creative and crazy as we choose. To quote Ansel Adams "We must remember that a photograph can hold just as much as we put into it and no one has ever approached the full possibilities of the medium."* Although not necessarily better, this shot is at least different from any other photograph of oystercatchers I've come across.*

*Ansel Adams, quoted in *The Art of Photography* (Alexandria, VA: Time-Life Books, 1971) p. 12.

33/Stilts in Tandem

This photograph of a mated pair of black-necked stilts was made from a blind placed about seven metres from their ground nest. Over the course of two hours I took about fifty pictures as these birds paraded about, trying to obtain an image that had graphic impact and also expressed the strong but invisible bond between the two stilts. The

black oystercatchers were photographed in a similar way. The lower camera angle of the picture creates a sense of openness and perspective. The strewn feathers—although originating from a gull—seem to trace the footsteps of the oystercatchers, giving emphasis to their passing.

Another drowsy half-hour passed before her plaintive cry floated in from the prairie. Immediately the young converged pell mell on the nest, staggering clumsily through the tangle of stems in their eagerness to be fed. They huddled together. Four pairs of keen eyes traced a circle in the sky and suddenly the big bird of prey dropped into the viewfinder. A tense, frozen silence took over as her blazing eyes surveyed the blind. I dared not breathe. Finally the fierce gaze shifted to the line of swaying, expectant hawklets and lunch began. Cautiously I started working the camera.

For photographing an extremely wary subject such as a marsh hawk, a blind is indispensable. It allows the photographer to record natural, intimate behaviour that will not normally go on in the presence of humans. Furthermore, photography can be carried out over a longer period of time without the animal becoming alarmed or taking flight, thus increasing the photographer's chances of obtaining an exceptional image.

A wild creature's inclination to accept a blind is not always a certainty. What one species tolerates may produce stark terror in a closely related one. There may also be great variation in individuals of the same species. At different times even a single animal may show great change in its attitude towards a blind. Generally, wild animals tend to be less cautious during their breeding season, or when they are hungry or tired. The success of a blind may be due just as often to finding an animal compatible with its use as it is to the method in which it is introduced and utilized by the photographer.

Making a Blind

The standard wildlife blind is a box-shaped structure made of fabric stretched over a wooden or metal framework large enough to conceal a seated photographer and his equipment. They are quite easy to build and several designs are included in this book. Although a blind is successful if it prevents wildlife from detecting the photographer's presence, there are a number of considerations to designing one that is enjoyable to use. (Fig. 4):

- EXPENSE—Spend as little money as possible to alleviate bothersome concerns over theft or vandalism to the blind during the long periods when it must be left unattended.
- PORTABILITY—Use lightweight materials. Sections of aluminum tubing (tent poles) are best for building the frame. Although cotton is not the lightest fabric available, it is best because it is easily repaired and altered with instant sewing glue. The blind needn't be large. For the average-sized 35-mm-camera user a floor area one metre square and a height of 1 1/2 metres (fabric dimensions) are ample. This size of blind would be similar in bulk to a two- or three-man backpacking tent.

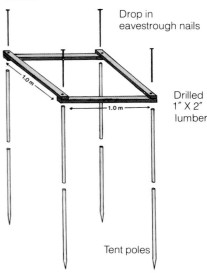

Figure 4
Building a Blind

Frame

Drop in eavestrough nails

1.0 m

1.0 m

Drilled 1" X 2" lumber

Tent poles

For portability leave all parts unattached

Fabric
(dull colour)

Stitch seams together

1.5 m

1.0 m

Figure 5
**The All-Purpose
Concertina Blind**

Materials: 5–6 yds. fabric (54″ width), contact cement, hula hoops, electrical tape.

1) Cut fabric into two equal-length pieces. These pieces should be 6 inches longer than your height.

2) Glue or stitch pieces together long side to long side to obtain one large piece.

3) Sew four equally spaced 2″ hems lengthwise. Use a hula hoop to trace out roof section.

4) Open hoops: Insert them into hems and refasten hoops with electrical tape.

5) Cut out and glue roof piece to wall section.

6) Cement open edges of fabric to close walls. Leave upper section open to accommodate camera.

- VERSATILITY—Don't sew permanent openings in the blind. Each situation usually requires a different positioning of the camera due to such factors as uneven terrain, or a badly placed tree limb. It's best to cut out the opening once the blind is erected. Thereafter, new openings may be cut as needed and old ones enlarged, altered or closed up. Peep-holes should also be cut in the sides and top of the blind so that the photographer can stay abreast of activity in the vicinity of the shooting site. Repairs and alterations can be made quite simply on the spot with a small knife and instant sewing glue.
- COLOUR—Try to match the colour of the fabric with the type of terrain in which the blind will be used. A camouflaged pattern is definitely best, not nearly so much to fool wildlife as to make the structure less noticeable to other people. A stream of curiosity-seekers investigating the blind will disturb the very wildlife one is trying to safeguard. Furthermore, a passer by may take a liking to the cute little tent and cart it home. If necessity forces the erection of a blind on a highly visible site, an intimidating sign such as "Danger: Sensitive Area. Harvard University Poisonous Snake Research in Progress. Do not Disturb" may help fend off unwanted visitors.

The Concertina Blind

I started using a concertina blind about ten years ago, specifically for mobility in photographing great blue herons feeding in shallow lakes and marshes. (Fig. 5.) However, there proved to be so many other advantages to the design that I now use it in almost any situation that calls for the use of a blind, be it in a tree, on the water, on a cliff or in an open field. It adjusts easily to a range of heights due to its accordion-like structure, allowing photography from standing, sitting or even prone positions. The circular shape makes it especially suitable for wind-swept terrains where flat-sided designs become unmanageable. It is light and easily portable, and sets up in a fraction of the time required by other types of blinds. It is also ideally suited for use in tidal areas, lakes and marshes, since the hoops float on the water's surface, permitting the height of the blind to adjust automatically to variations in water levels that occur during stalking or tide changes.

Materials for this blind are inexpensive. A rubber-backed, lightweight nylon fabric is recommended because of its water-shedding properties. This material is available in most fabric shops in a variety of colours—usually even an olive-drab camouflage pattern. The exercise hoops used for support can be purchased in department stores. Failing this, plumbing-supply stores stock flexible plastic pipe ideal for the purpose. A sewing machine is necessary for the assembly and as long as one can sew in a straight line the job can be completed in an afternoon.

Motion:
Flowing and Frozen

34/Skeins of Sandhill Cranes
Every year during the first week of September tens of thousands of giant sandhill cranes gather to rest and feed on the shores of Last Mountain Lake in central Saskatchewan. In a few weeks the cranes have moved on toward their tropical American wintering ground, but during that brief sojourn they present a spectacle to thrill the soul of any nature lover, a timeless scene that is enhanced by the prairie's austere beauty. This image is the product of two photographs taken moments apart and later sandwiched together. In making the composite I chose to have the two flocks flying in opposite directions to play upon the "heads and tails" irony that is evident in the nearer group of birds.

35/Dowitcher Flock in Flight
Wobbling out into the middle of a prairie slough inside a portable blind may appear strange to a passing motorist but it is an effective technique for approaching birds. On this occasion there were many small flocks of shorebirds foraging over a stretch of mudflats. Some took exception to my intrusion and wheeled about the blind. I made this picture at 1/15 second while panning with the flock. Stationary elements (background) were consequently blurred and the bodies of the birds remained relatively sharp. Notice how the flow of movement toward the open space extends the free-and-easy feeling of the image.

Stationary Use

If the photographic site is in an open area, the first step is simply to lay the blind in the correct position. The three support poles (two-section aluminum tent poles are best) are driven into the ground about the blind's periphery. Thereafter the blind may be raised inside the poles as the animal grows accustomed to its presence. The entire structure is suspended by tying the uppermost hoop to the poles with wire. In a wooded area or in a tree above the ground, the blind can be suspended from a convenient branch by a cord or wire fastened to the uppermost hoop. The bottom may be anchored with rocks or pegs, or tacked to the support platform in the case of an in-tree site.

Mobile Use

One of the important features of the concertina blind is its easy adaptability to mobile use—a decided advantage in photographing animals whose movements are unpredictable. (Fig. 6) The photographer can adjust his position at will to gain a more favourable background, better lighting, an improved shooting angle or a change in subject magnification. Converting the blind to mobile use is accomplished by means of a harness made from household materials. (Fig. 7) This harness allows the blind to be supported on the back of the photographer. The unwieldy nature of a tripod makes it

Figure 6
Using the Mobile Blind

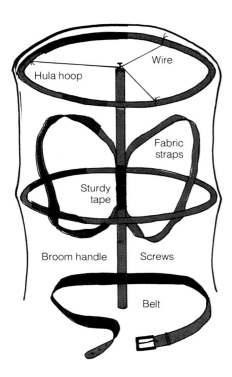

Figure 7
Concertina Harness

Hula hoop

Wire

Fabric straps

Sturdy tape

Broom handle

Screws

Belt

impractical for use in the blind when one is stalking. A monopod, or better still, a simple wooden bipod equipped with a ball-and-socket head will help support and steady the camera. When the terrain permits, I try to shoot from a kneeling position. This improves camera steadiness and the bipod is built to work at this height.

Blinds from Natural Cover

There are occasional situations when natural cover can be used to disguise the photographer's presence. In northern regions, blocks of snow roofed over with a tarpaulin or ground sheet can be used for concealment near a carcass or other bait attractive to foxes, wolves, coyotes, bears, ravens, eagles and other scavengers. In marshy areas a heavy clump of bullrushes or cattails can be bent over and tied together at the top to form a teepee-like structure that will effectively shield the photographer from birds in the water as well as those overhead. Brush, log piles, trees, stones, bales of hay and haystacks, and simple earthen excavations may serve as blinds, especially when used in conjunction with materials, such as boards or tarpaulins, supplied by the photographer.

I once located a prairie falcon eyrie at the entrance to a small cave located high on a rock face. The terrain made the erection of a blind impossible. However, I was able to climb right past the startled nestlings and set up my equipment in the rear of the cave behind a sheet suspended from the rock overhead. Although the quarters were cramped, I was able to photograph the feeding activities successfully at a distance of less than two metres without alarming the parents. The sounds made by these powerful birds of prey—the hysterical food cries of the young, the terrible screams of the adults, the snap of bone and tearing of fur and flesh as the prey was dismembered at feeding time, all amplified by the acoustical properties of the cave itself—were more memorable to me than the actual photography. This was carried out in near darkness using electronic flash.

It is rare, however, for natural cover to be much more than a compromise to be used when a bona fide blind cannot be precisely situated.

Man-made Structures as Blinds

Houses and tool sheds may provide good vantage points for photographing bird nests or wildlife that is attracted to a feeding station. **(48)(49)** In such cases shooting should not be done through glass unless it is a single sheet of good quality. Often an ordinary tent can be pressed into service as a blind for ground subjects. Boats, canoes, kayaks or other watercraft can be used to achieve a close approach to waterfowl, sea mammals, moose, turtles and other water-loving creatures, especially if the photographer takes steps to disguise his presence.

Rare Encounters in the Field

36/Yipping Coyote

Whenever I set out on a photographic excursion, I try to have at least one definite goal in mind. It might be the intention to shoot a specific subject, to investigate a certain quality of light or colour, or to explore a theme such as "winter moods". This charges the foray with a sense of purpose and keeps me motivated. Despite these intentions, I try to remain alert to unforeseen opportunities that could make the trip additionally rewarding. Not all such accidental discoveries are as dramatic as a crooning coyote, but a natural design or pattern of colour that excites the imagination may just as easily lead to artistically satisfying images. I was sitting in a blind near a Saskatchewan slough when this coyote showed up. No doubt attracted by the abundance of recently hatched shorebirds and waterfowl that were scampering through the reeds and sedges, it came directly toward me across a field without becoming alarmed. Drawing closer it seemed to catch my scent, then stiffened, let out a few yips and carried on with its business, creating quite a commotion as it worked its way around the pothole.

The Car as a Blind

Many kinds of wildlife show little fear of automobiles. They are especially effective as blinds because they can be moved at will to follow an animal or gain a better camera angle. In most of North America motorized vehicles are required to stay on established roadways. Setting off crosscountry in pursuit of a grazing mule deer is not possible. Although I have seen in recent years some photographs that are the products of a photographer using a snowmobile to chase wildlife until it becomes so disoriented and exhausted that it is easily photographed, the practice is nevertheless illegal, not to mention ruthless and inhumane.

Fortunately, the brushy cover that grows commonly along rural roadsides is attractive to wildlife and presents frequent opportunities for picture-taking to the vehicle-bound photographer. A 400- or 500-mm lens is needed for the many types of birds that feed, nest or sing in roadside habitats. To obtain sharp pictures, such a lens must be attached to a firm support. Car window telescope mounts used by birdwatchers and sold commercially are also quite appropriate for telephoto photography, provided the tripod mount on the lens barrel can be revolved to permit levelling of the camera when the car is parked on a slope. A custom-made window mount can be fashioned less expensively using wood clamps and some small pieces of lumber to make a platform onto which a ball-and-socket head can be attached. In my own vehicle I took the legs off a worn-out tripod and bolted what was left to the inside of the car door. The tripod head and post are kept out of the way under the driver's seat, ready to be slipped into the centre column when required. When shooting with a long lens inside a car, keep in mind that even slight movements in the car will jar the vehicle enough to cause unacceptable camera vibrations. It is wise to keep a couple of old towels handy in the car to hang over the windows so that the occupants will not inadvertently frighten the subject.

Photographing birds and mammals from a car is exciting, fast-paced and not physically demanding, but it usually yields rather mediocre picture results. The camera angle is often too high to capture intimate views of subjects at ground level. Many animals will flee as soon as the car engine is stopped (a necessity to avoid camera shake) and a shot or two, quickly made, is usually all that is possible. However, it is fun, and the excellent pictures that occasionally result can make it a worthwhile endeavour from a photographic standpoint as well.

Blinds in Trees and on Cliffs

Sometimes the photographer will find it necessary to construct a blind in a hazardous location such as in a tree or on a cliff. The main safety precaution is not to work alone. In recent years several wildlife photographers have died primarily because help could not be summoned when it was needed. If there is any danger of falling, a safety rope should be used. It should be tied around the upper body underneath the armpits and fastened to a firm support, with only a metre or so of play in the line to allow freedom of movement.

First Flight

One of my first attempts at wildlife photography involved shooting a nesting colony of great blue herons. A friend and I had built a platform blind about twenty-five metres above the ground in a large sugar maple that stood in the middle of the wooded swamp where the colony was located. Climbing up to the platform one day to take my shift I noticed that the herons were circling about at close range, anxious for us to disappear so they could return to their nests. We had an aluminum lawn chair in the blind and I crawled in and settled back without checking things thoroughly. What I failed to notice was that the rear legs of the chair had shifted off the platform, although the fabric wall of the blind still held the chair upright. I sat down and leaned back and suddenly the sky and branches overhead were doing somersaults and I was flailing frantically for something to grab onto. Fortunately I managed to hook one arm over a branch after falling only a couple of metres. The danger was not as great as it seems for even though it was far too slack, I had remembered to fasten the safety rope before sitting down. But the experience was unnerving and the flying lesson has never been forgotten.

When working in trees, the photographer often has a problem getting up a trunk devoid of handholds. A simple, safe method for the part-time climber involves using thirteen- to sixteen-centimetre spikes and a climbers' safety belt (available at safety supply stores). The spikes are driven into the trunk with a hammer, to serve as footholds. A rope is looped about the trunk and fastened to the climbers' belt in typical lumberjack fashion. Then, leaning back against the rope the climber works his way up the trunk driving in the spikes where necessary. It's a slower but safer process than using climbing spurs. The spikes are left in the trunk and do not leave wounds which can allow the entry of disease. As soon as possible a safety rope should be thrown over a sturdy limb to protect the climber from a possible fall.

Building a Platform

Constructing a blind in a tree begins with wiring the supporting members of the platform to favourably situated limbs. Several lengths of lumber (38 × 86 mm—2 × 4″—stock is adequate) fastened with nails or wire are sufficient to provide a sturdy, supporting framework. Then boards or plywood may be nailed in place to form the floor. Thereafter the blind can be erected in the normal way.

Insects
on the Move

37/Bee Fly Diving for Nectar
Observing the behaviour of these flies for a few minutes while they foraged over a patch of flowers, I discovered that on approaching a blossom they stopped abruptly and hovered momentarily in mid-air before dropping into the flower. Further, they appeared to work their way over the blooms in a predictable, systematic manner. Up went the tripod; out came the camera, a 200-mm lens and an extension tube; I knelt down behind the apparatus ready for action. In one fortunate shot out of about twenty exposures, I caught the animal diving headlong at a shutter speed of 1/500 second. The trailing legs are used as air rudders.

38/Butterfly Warming Up
*Like the bee fly, this butterfly was shot
under natural light. The high degree of
magnification inherent in insect photography severely limits the depth of field
and leaves little room for focusing error.
However, in this situation, sharpness
was not my goal. I was more interested
in the out-of-focus, muted colour
pattern of the background. It formed a
harmonious backdrop for the butterfly
as it warmed its wings in the early
morning sun, enhancing the light
feeling of the image. The soft blurring of
the wings resulted from a relatively slow
shutter speed of 1/30 second.*

When evaluating a tree site for possible photography, look for a favourable arrangement of limbs, either in the same tree as the nest, if it is a large deciduous species, or in an adjacent one which provides suitable magnification, lighting and camera angle. In groves of small trees several trunks may be used simultaneously to support the platform bridgework.

Wind becomes a considerable problem in tree blinds. The photographer should make sure that the blind frame is well guyed to nearby limbs and that the fabric is stretched tightly and tacked down so that it does not move about and frighten the birds. Even in light winds, the entire platform may sway, making focusing and framing very difficult. In some cases the problem may be alleviated by joining the platform to the nest site with lumber so that they move in unison.

Cliff Blinds

For setting up a blind on precipitous, rocky terrain, a platform is not usually needed. Often there are sufficient crevices into which the support poles of the blind may be jammed and they can subsequently be guyed with wire to pitons or perhaps just to convenient rock projections. Frequently a full blind is not needed and the photographer can couch himself in a recess of the cliff-face, shielding the open side with fabric. For a cliff location he has not yet seen, the concertina blind is the most suitable. It requires only a minimum of auxiliary support (sometimes one pole is sufficient) and its circular shape makes it especially wind resistant.

Blinds in the Water

In most situations involving wetland wildlife, the water will be shallow enough to set up the blind in the usual way, although longer poles may be required in marshes where the bottom is very soft. Chest waders are worn while the photographer is seated in the blind. In deeper water a flat-bottomed boat can be anchored securely in shooting position and a blind fashioned inside the boat. The tripod should be located so that the photographer can sit or kneel on the bottom of the boat, not only for added stability, but also to provide a good camera angle for animals at water level. For photography at a nest site, a second boat may be needed to transport the photographer to the boat that must remain stationed at the nest.

Muskrat Mania

Sometimes blinds deliver far more than the photographer bargains for. One autumn I photographed a muskrat lodge while lying on top of a slab of styrofoam that I had floated into position. I was hidden by a makeshift blind, and a very aromatic heap of roadside weeds that had been added to complete the camouflage. Six or seven fat muskrats were loafing about the lodge, scratching, grooming and enjoying the morning sunshine. As I drew closer the usual signs of nervousness began to show. Beady-eyed stares and nostril twitching spread up and down the line of rats and soon two or three plunged into the concealing depths of the slough. However, to my surprise they immediately surfaced even closer to me. My astonishment turned to nervousness as I heard and felt their claws scratching at the platform. Then a soggy rat appeared on the deck right in front of me. Still hidden by the blind I was fairly sure that once the significance of my scent dawned on these dull-witted rodents they would retreat to a more respectful distance. (I couldn't even take pictures as they were much closer than the lens would focus.) Then another appeared and briefly inspected the lens protruding from the blind. Both animals seemed quite taken with the weedy camouflage, pawing through the pile with great interest. Then I felt something moving along my back and the next thing I knew a set of dewy whiskers was peeking up at me from beneath my armpit. So much for respecting my scent. They had the run of the blind and platform for about ten minutes. I remained quite still the whole time, having read stories of muskrats occasionally turning aggressive. It was when they started to pile pondweeds inside, intending to move in permanently, that I decided to clear out, and as I eased away they went overboard and back to their own lodge.

Machinations
in a Spring Meadow

39/Long-jawed Spider in Ambush
Poised inconspicuously on a camas bud, this spider is keeping a concerned eye or two on its nearby web. Should an animal become entangled, it would close immediately, looping silk over its victim to ensure the capture. Later the spider will inject digestive enzymes directly into the prey enabling it to pump out and consume the animal's interior. Hunkered within inches of this wisp of life, intent on the drama, is a huge, 65-kg mammal—me. It's easy to lose oneself in the fascination of nature's micro world. Many pleasant, productive hours may be spent simply lying around in a meadow. What at first may seem devoid of activity soon begins to pulse with life once the photographer lowers himself into the grass and reins in his perceptions. By using natural light in this picture, I was able to record on film the rich hues and intriguing depth of the setting, a faithful rendering of the scene's atmosphere and vibrancy that would be difficult to duplicate if electronic flash were used. The camera was motor-driven and mounted on an ankle-high monopod. Automatic film advance is a boon to macrophotography where critical framing is disturbed if the film is wound manually.

CHAPTER TWO

The Allure of the Bird

Except for himself, no life form has captured more of man's interest than the bird. Considered the most beautiful, graceful and melodious of the vertebrates, they are watched, studied and admired in all corners of the globe. They have adapted to most of the earth's environments—desert, jungle, polar ice-cap, suburban backyard, sewage pond and urban centre—providing the wildlife photographer with a ready abundance of subjects. I have photographed birds at all times of the day and in every season—owls after dark, swans migrating in the fall, cardinals at winter feeders, golden eagles during the spring nesting season, and herons fishing during the heat of summer.

Consider also the photogenic aspects of the animal itself—its casual but magnificent beauty when airborne and the rich, striking colour of its plumage. The supple, sinewy nature of its skeletal structure allows the animal to present a variety of intriguing poses. The spectacle of massed migrations, the bizarre courtship rituals, the many methods of obtaining food, nest-building, and rearing the young, the first flight—all are small but compelling natural dramas to excite the photographer's imagination. Also, almost anywhere one lives in North America there are scores of species within walking distance of home.

Understanding Bird Behaviour

Successful bird photography begins with an understanding of the behaviour of the bird itself. Although visually beautiful, birds are not exactly gifted in the intellectual department. For the most part they are incapable of even elementary reasoning, their activities being governed by instinct. They are programmed to react in a certain way when confronted by certain stimuli regardless of the situation. The behaviour patterns that result appear complex, but they nevertheless allow the photographer to predict and even direct bird activity to his advantage.

Two aspects of bird behaviour are most significant to the photographer—food procurement and the reproductive cycle. Each of North America's approximately one thousand species has a unique way of carrying out these activities. It's not possible for a photographer to keep this information in his head. In fact, accurate life histories for many species have not yet been recorded. However, a general knowledge of this behaviour is required, as well as a familiarity with the published literature in order to obtain special information when required.

To illustrate this point, consider a typical series of events that would occur in photographing a bird at the nest. A photographer, out for a hike in the spring, glimpses a bird carrying something—possibly a twig, an insect or even a bit of fluff. From experience he realizes immediately that the bird is probably heading directly for the nest. When he locates the nest, he finds it is that of a chipping sparrow and contains two eggs. The site being suitable for photography, a course of action is planned. In order not to jeopardize the bird's reproductive activities, correct timing of the working sessions is essential. To do this the photographer must find out how many eggs a chipping sparrow lays, the duration of the incubation period and how long the young will remain in the nest after hatching. He may also wish to learn of any behaviour quirks of the species that might influence his photographic approach. Most of this information will be obtained by consulting specialized literature.

There are of course many books that deal with bird life in a general way and the photographer will want to become familiar with the material they cover. When more specialized information is required, especially in regard to nesting behaviour, two common references may be consulted. They are *Life Histories of Birds of North America* (20 volumes) by Arthur Cleveland Bent (New York: Dover Publications) and *The Audubon Society Encyclopaedia of North American Birds* by John K. Terres (New York: Alfred A. Knopf Inc., 1980).

Birds at the Nest

A blind is usually necessary for photographing the nesting activity of most birds. Some species, however, have no natural fear of humans and concealment is not required. For instance, colonial nesting seabirds (auks, puffins, murres, gannets) reproduce on remote islands devoid of ground predators and an instinctive fear of mammals has never become part of their behaviour pattern. Some individuals are so rigidly programmed to carry out the reproductive cycle that normal fear reactions are suppressed. At times such birds may be picked up by hand from the nest. At other times they will feed their young no matter where they may be, even perched on the photographer's finger. As a general rule, the smaller the bird is, the more likely it is to be at ease in the presence of humans. Birds the size of warblers, hummingbirds and chickadees can be photographed without the encumbrance of a blind. (7) Occasionally even a large species such as the pileated woodpecker will show little fear of humans.

While visiting the Birds of Prey Natural Area in Idaho's Snake River valley, I came upon the nest of a ferruginous hawk, a large prairie raptor well known for its fierce defense of its breeding territory. Typical members of the species, they had built the nest on an open rock prominence at the top of a canyon wall—almost on the prairie itself. The adult bird was on the nest shading the four downy young from the sun's burning rays. Surprisingly, she continued this behaviour even when I approached within twenty metres. Had I put her off the nest, I would have had to retreat immediately to safeguard the vulnerable young. For two hours there was not a sound, nor any movement, just the energy of the wind moving over the rocks, the stark, hot light and the tension that flowed between me and the bird. As I expected, the pictures were boring but the experience itself unforgettable. Ten days later when the young were much stronger, I returned, erected a blind during which time the parents repeatedly buzzed me, and succeeded in obtaining some satisfying photographs. (40)

Bird Safety First

The first rule of bird photography is to do nothing that will jeopardize either the health of the bird or the success of the reproductive cycle. For one thing dead birds and abandoned nests simply aren't the stuff of which great nature photographs are made. Good pictures result when wildlife is oblivious to, or uninterested in, the photographer's presence, allowing him ample time to develop a creative approach to the situation. Rushing into an area, crowding and frightening an animal, usually results in no pictures at all, or at best one or two ill-conceived snapshots. Fortunately, the endearing qualities of the subject matter have a way of ensuring its welfare when it is confronted by a curious nature photographer. Who could step on an orchid after wrestling with its graceful curves in the viewfinder for an hour? What photographer would not grow apprehensive for the safety of a litter of clumsy coyote pups romping innocently before the camera?

Problems that do arise are generally caused by a lack of awareness of potential hazards rather than a lack of concern. I was once escorted to the site of an avocet colony, my first visit to such a place. Becoming excited with the photographic possibilities of one nest, I neglected to watch where I was walking and stepped almost immediately into an adjacent one, destroying two of the three eggs. The experience completely dampened my enthusiasm for the project, which I abandoned, in truth feeling quite hypocritical and guilty in the presence of those particular birds. We placed the remaining egg in another nest as we were sure the "oaf-trodden" nest would be abandoned.

The photographer should be sure to study carefully the natural history of potentially sensitive subjects to minimize the possibility of disturbance. A field researcher at the Birds of Prey Natural Area in Idaho told me that some golden eagles are likely to abandon a nest simply because a vehicle passes through a valley below the eyrie.

Finding Bird Nests

One necessary task for the bird photographer is finding a suitable nest at which to work. Most birds, especially ground-nesting species, are adept at concealing the structure to protect it from such predators as squirrels, raccoons, foxes, jays, gulls, and snakes. Although one's initial attempts at nest-finding may be frustrating, it becomes easier with experience. An enjoyable and exciting task, it is nevertheless time-consuming. Valuable information, which may save considerable time and effort, can be obtained from birdwatchers, naturalists, farmers, foresters and other people who spend a lot of time outside.

A basic ability to identify birds (both male and female of the species) and a familiarity with their habitat preferences are prerequisites to successful nest-finding. To accomplish this a field guide is necessary and at present there is only one you need to consider buying: *A Guide to Field Identification—Birds of North America* by Chandler S. Robbins and others (New York: Golden Press, 1966).

Strategies

There are two basic approaches to finding bird nests. The stationary method involves taking up a position that offers an unobstructed view of the area under study. The observer should survey the scene with the aid of binoculars, keeping alert for any of the following behaviour:

- A singing male indicates breeding activity for that species. A nest is almost surely nearby or in the stages of construction.
- The repeated appearance of a bird at the same location.
- The swift, direct flight of a bird into thick vegetation may indicate it is following a well-travelled pathway to the nest.
- A number of birds hovering or circling in the same area may indicate a breeding colony.
- A bird carrying anything is usually *en route* to its nest. Mark the landing spot carefully and keep it under surveillance.

Delay making an actual search of the suspect area until you are sure of the evidence.

The second method entails active searching. It is most effective when done with a partner, each person being able to spot the birds that are scared off the nest by the other. A pole about two metres long will aid in the search. In marshes, it can be used to check water depths and maintain balance. However, its primary benefit comes from waving it over the tops of grasses, sedges, cattails and other ground cover as one moves along. This causes nesting birds to fly up when normally they would remain frozen and unseen even though the searcher passes close by. In a grassland habitat a searcher can cover an area four or five metres wide as he moves down the field. The pole also assists in carefully parting branches to peer into thickets and other dense cover. Naturally, the types of clues outlined in the stationary method should be given the necessary attention by the searcher, but most finds will be the result of birds that are frightened off the nest. If one is working with a partner, a light rope twenty or thirty metres long may be stretched between the two people and dragged across the grasstops while the searchers remain alert for any explosions of flight.

When a nest is found, its location should be carefully noted by using available landmarks, or by creating one, with a rock, log or stick, so that later, no time is lost refinding the nest. The photographer should note the species and number of eggs or age of nestlings, quickly but thoroughly analyze the suitability of the site for photography, and then remove himself from the area. Time spent in the vicinity of the nest should be kept to a minimum, especially if incubation is still in progress.

The Photogenic Nest

Only a few of the nests located will be suitable for photography. The first consideration is the feasibility of building a blind. At many sites, especially those in trees or on cliffs, a blind is not practical. Lighting is also important. If the photographer can set up to the south of the nest, a variety of lighting types may be utilized, including front, side, and partial-back, as well as diffused overcast illumination should it occur. The background is as important a consideration as any. It will establish to a great degree the over-all mood of the photographs. I prefer open backgrounds with strong colour, an effect which is achieved when the foliage or landscape is far enough behind the nest so that it can be thrown out of focus by the use of a large aperture. For the same reason I prefer nests that can be shot against the skyline.

A related concern is the immediate environment around the nest that will be included in the picture. Usually branches, leaves or grasses will obscure the nest. This material must not be removed as it protects the nest from sun, wind, precipitation and predators. However, it can be tied back out of view during the photography. This should be done in a manner that will appear natural and lend itself to good composition. Finally, the nest should not be in a location where the erection of a blind would draw the attention of a lot of people. Such a site, if used, is doomed to failure, both photographically and biologically.

Where to Look

Marginal habitats will generally offer the greatest variety and number of nests. These are areas where forest meets scrubland, scrubland meets meadow, meadow meets marsh and so on. By concentrating a variety of habitats in a small zone, such "edge" areas can support a wide spectrum of bird life. These habitat gradients almost always occur in the vicinity of streams, lakes and marshes, which is one reason why bodies of water are usually associated with a rich variety of fauna.

The Breeding Cycle

Successful bird photography depends on having a good knowledge of avian reproductive habits. Although there exist significant variations in the breeding cycle of birds, generally it follows a standard pattern. Described below is the process for an average-sized songbird (cardinal, starling, wood thrush).

The first phase, called "territoriality," begins in the spring as males of each species attempt to establish their personal breeding domains. This is by and large accomplished by singing and a showing of feathers, the loudest, most conspicuous and most persistent members of each species winning the territory. (1) The size of a territory may vary from a couple of acres (small songbirds) to a hundred or more square kilometres (golden eagles).

While the territorial jousts are still in progress a female is attracted and the second phase—courtship and nest-building—commences. One or both parents, depending on the species, may take part in the nest construction. For songbirds this phase lasts about two weeks and is ended by the laying of the eggs, usually carried out on a schedule of one a day or one every two days.

Each of the next two stages—incubation and care of the nestlings— lasts about two weeks. (45) For larger birds these stages will be considerably longer. (California condor young do not leave the nest until they are seven months old.) The young of some species are precocial, being fully feathered and able to walk soon after hatching. Such birds (shorebirds, gallinaceous birds, waterfowl) have a longer incubation period than one would expect for their size and the nest is abandoned soon after all the eggs are hatched. On leaving the nest most young continue to be fed by the parents for a period of time similar to their stay in the nest.

Keep in mind that there are as many variations, some subtle, others quite dramatic, as there are species. The photographer must familiarize himself thoroughly with the natural history of a species before undertaking to photograph it at the nest.

Working at the Nest

The timing of the commencement of work at the nest is governed by the breeding cycle of the bird itself. As a general rule, the more time and energy a bird has invested in a particular nest, the less likely it will be to abandon the site. Thus, photography begun during the nest-building or incubation stages will usually cause the bird to desert. Nor is human activity about the nest advisable immediately on hatching. A freshly hatched bird is not able to sustain a constant body temperature until its metabolism has stabilized and the down has grown in. In the meantime they must be brooded constantly by the parents.

For most songbirds the initial introduction of the blind must be delayed until four or five days after all the eggs have hatched. At this stage, activity about the nest is quite intense, remaining so until the young are fledged and providing the photographer with ample opportunities for exciting shooting.

The nests of large birds of prey should be left undisturbed for a longer period (ten days to two weeks). At this time photography at the nest is ideal as prey is frequently brought to the nest, dismembered and fed to the young. (40) After five or six weeks the hawklets begin to feed themselves and the adult birds appear for only brief periods of time, making photographic prospects less attractive.

Birds which hatch precocial young must of course be photographed during the incubation period. Fortunately, these species are not readily kept off the nest and adjust quickly to the presence of a blind if it is properly introduced. (44)(33) By starting work late in the incubation period, the photographer not only shows necessary caution but also has an opportunity to obtain rare photographs of the hatching process, and the young and parents together before they leave the site.

Introducing the Blind

Setting up a blind at a bird nest should be done as expeditiously as possible. A well-thought-out plan, tight organization, and a thorough preparation of materials should be made before entering the nesting territory to minimize the length of time the bird is to be kept off the nest. The disturbance should usually not exceed fifteen minutes. In extreme weather conditions no work should be attempted.

For me, the first step is usually setting up the camera and tripod in its working location, being careful to obtain the desired shooting angle and subject magnification. An object approximating the size of the adult birds is set on or near the nest to assist in framing the scene. Once the camera position is precisely determined, I construct the blind around it.

Erect Blind in Stages

To allow the bird to adjust gradually to its presence, the blind should be erected in stages. (Fig. 8) The first step is usually a matter of driving in the lower sections of the support poles and spreading the fabric on the ground inside them. If this is done in the early morning, by afternoon the photographer may return and drape the fabric over the poles so that the blind attains half of its normal size. In the same way the top half of the poles may be added and the fabric stretched to full size in two stages on the second day. During this final stage of construction, the tripod should be set up inside the blind (if there is no danger of theft) and a dummy lens—made of a cardboard tube of appropriate size and colour—installed to protrude from the blind's opening.

Be sure that the blind is well guyed in windy areas. The fabric should never be allowed to flap as this can be very upsetting to some birds. Bits of the surrounding vegetation should be pressed into service as extra camouflage, provided this does not lead to property damage. While working, the photographer should take precautions not to create any trails which might lead predators to the nest.

Reactions of the Bird

At each stage of blind construction the photographer, on leaving the scene, should observe from a distance the behaviour of the subjects, to judge whether or not his recent work is acceptable to them. If the timing is correct most birds will return to the nest with little if any hesitation. If fear of the blind is shown and the bird does not return, no time should be wasted in removing or partially disassembling the structure. If the bird still appears upset the project should be abandoned altogether and the photographer should attempt to find a more confiding bird. Fifteen minutes is ample time for most species to settle down. Large raptors may remain away for several hours at a stretch as a normal course of events when the young have begun feeding themselves. Such situations should be judged accordingly.

Just as some birds may be photographed at the nest without a blind others may adjust to the presence of a fully constructed blind almost immediately, saving the photographer the longer process of introducing it in stages. However, it is not easy to prejudge a bird's reaction, and caution is always the wisest course. Often, birds that are very aggressive toward the photographer will settle down quickly once he has departed, regardless of the size of the structure left in his wake. High-tree nesters are usually more leery of a blind than birds that nest on or near the ground.

Birds Can Count

When the time arrives to begin taking pictures, an assistant is required, to

Figure 8
**Introducing the Blind
Static Method**

141

accompany the photographer to the site. Once final adjustments are made and the photographer is settled, the accomplice leaves, holding aloft a hanger bearing a shirt similar to the one worn by the photographer in order to simulate the departure of both individuals. Although this procedure may seem a little ridiculous, most birds will not return until they think all visitors have left the area. It is of no avail to enter the blind before daybreak as the sound of the arrival will be both heard and seen, and duly noted. It may be possible in some cases to sneak into the blind undetected while the parents are out hunting, especially with species that forage far afield. When the shooting session is over the assistant should return, scaring the bird from the immediate vicinity so that it will not see the photographer exit the blind and thereby associate the structure directly with people.

Inside the Blind

Waiting for the bird to make its first visit to the nest while one is hiding inside the blind is very exciting, but it is important not to rush things once the subject arrives. The initial visit should be allowed to pass without the sound of an operating camera adding to the bird's nervousness. On the subsequent visit the first few exposures should be made tentatively without the use of a motor drive, allowing the bird to resettle completely between each shot. Fortunately, most birds quickly become accustomed to the sound of a camera (even motor-driven ones) and pay it little notice thereafter.

Light in the Forest

For me natural light is the ideal type of illumination at the nest. However, pictures taken at sites in the forest shade will have a green cast, due to the filtration effect of the foliage. Although our eyes adjust automatically to the imbalance, the warm colours in particular will lose their richness and vibrancy in the resulting image. As the plumages of many forest nesters are dominated by reds, browns and oranges, it is important that these colours be rendered accurately. A + 5 magenta filter can be used to bring the light back into proper balance.

Hollywood Woods

The use of electronic flash in the forest setting is a very attractive alternative. Flash is correctly balanced for daylight film. It is of short duration and thus can freeze the quick movements of small birds. The photographer can use any aperture he desires, simply by adjusting the flash-to-subject distance. The main drawback is the artificial impression it leaves on the picture. However, there are several ways in which the image can take on a more natural feeling.

The photographer should try to illuminate all parts of the scene evenly so that there is no obvious light fall-off in the picture's background. This can be done by keeping all picture elements equidistant from the main flash, or flashes if more than one are required. He should locate the main illumination in a position other than that which would produce frontal lighting—preferably to the side or even behind the subject to produce a more candid, just-found impression. Fill-in illumination is certainly necessary to counteract the characteristic harshness of electronic flash. However, I would not locate the fill unit in the standard on-camera position; this is not only an unnatural origin for fill light but it will also produce a "Hollywood" glitter in the bird's eye. (Any eye highlights should be made by the main light.) Instead, locate the fill light well below the camera-subject axis, approximately opposite the main illumination and two and one half to three times farther from the subject than the main light. (Alternatively, cut down the power of the fill light by two and one half to three stops.) Finally I would locate the lights at a distance that would permit the use of an aperture that would produce only moderate depth of field, so that the image does not show the all-encompassing sharpness typical of electronic flash work.

For the photographer still looking for his first bird nest, these lighting procedures might seem unduly sophisticated. However, in the past, the standard, in-studio, human-portrait lighting arrangement has been widely used to photograph birds at the nest. This often results in pictures that look as if they were shot on the backlot at MGM. The suggestions above are only logically derived from the way natural sunlight illuminates a forest setting.

Photography in a Bird Box

Flickers, bluebirds, kestrels, tree swallows, purple martins and house wrens are a few of the birds that can be photographed inside nesting boxes. (Fig. 9) Each species has particular needs regarding the size of the entrance hole and the over-all dimensions of its house, factors which must be kept in mind when building the box. For photographic purposes the top and back of the structure must be easily removable; this is most conveniently accomplished by the use of screws in the assembly. Once the eggs have hatched and the parents are bringing food to the young, the photographer merely substitutes a different back and top panel, the new walls being fitted with a camera and electronic flash unit. Completed in only a few minutes, this trick goes unnoticed by the birds in the dim interior of the box. A wide-angle lens with a close-up supplementary lens can be used to provide a full view of the activity within the cramped quarters. The shutter is tripped remotely (from concealment if necessary) once the parent is seen

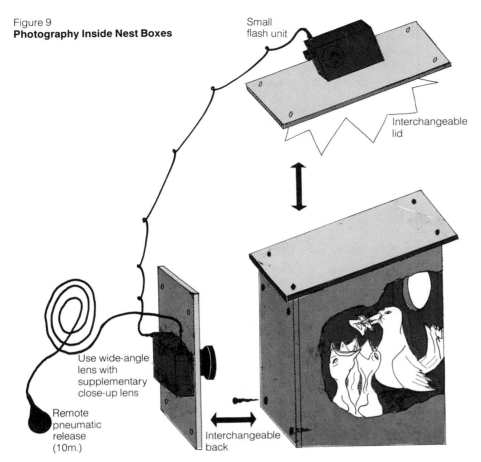

Figure 9
Photography Inside Nest Boxes

Small flash unit

Interchangeable lid

Use wide-angle lens with supplementary close-up lens

Remote pneumatic release (10m.)

Interchangeable back

to enter the box. Ideally the film can be advanced with a motor drive; if the photographer is advancing the film manually, he should do it between feedings, provided this activity is not upsetting to the birds. Lighting is supplied by the flash unit fitted to the roof panel. Its intensity can be controlled by covering the reflector with paper diffusers. Automatic flashes should perform perfectly provided the sensor is not obscured.

Birds in the Field

There is an appealingly unpredictable aspect to bird photography away from the nest. Inasmuch as there are fewer natural controls that can be employed to control bird activity, it is difficult to forecast just what the shooting session might entail as to the subject matter or its behaviour. (36)

There are many types of locations where birds congregate regularly, and these are of significance to the photographer. Dancing grounds or "leks" are special areas where some species of birds (grouse in particular) gather for courtship display and copulation. The courting arenas vary from thirty to several hundred metres in extent and can be easily defined and exploited by the photographer, especially if a blind is cautiously introduced. The ruffed grouse is another special case. The male enacts its spectacular, solo, springtime "drumming" display on a specific stump or forest log. In tidal areas many species (shorebirds, gulls, terns, cormorants) have favoured roosting sites on rocks that remain unflooded at high tide. (32) Here they can be stalked, or, better still, photographed from a blind.

Stalking Birds in the Concertina Blind

It is not easy to sneak up on a bird no matter how quiet or well camouflaged one attempts to be. Unless a bird is strongly attracted to a specific location, there is little chance of its staying around while a large earthy-looking creature slowly and painfully slithers toward it.

Success is more likely if the photographer can make the stalk inside a blind. As stated previously, cars and boats work well in this respect as they can glide almost imperceptibly over the landscape, but they are limited by their size and the nature of the terrain.

Stalking with the concertina blind in its mobile mode often yields excellent results. The photographer should put on the blind out of sight of the quarry. Before setting out, he should plan his approach, taking into account the lighting, the nature of the terrain, and possible obstacles to be avoided. A course should not ordinarily be set that will cut off an animal's escape route as this will make it nervous and more likely to take flight early. (20) With the photographer dressed in chest waders, the blind is ideally suited for stalking in lakes and marshes, where, in waist-deep water, he can walk comfortably upright while presenting only a small silhouette to the bird. (12) The hollow hoop ribs float on the water's surface and adjust to changes in depth.

The stalk itself must be slow and deliberate. Stop if the animal seems suspicious. Proceed when it resumes feeding, sleeping or other normal behaviour.

Reading the Quarry

When dealing with a very nervous subject, one should approach only until the subject becomes aware of the blind but does not yet show sign of real alarm, usually evidenced by raised head, stiff neck, staring or vocalization. This point may be considered the outer limit of the animal's safety zone. If the blind remains quite still on the periphery for thirty to forty-five minutes, the animal will come to accept it as part of the environment. Thereafter the photographer can move with less caution at closer range. Neglecting this procedure will cause many stalks to end in failure.

Using Bait

Although a bird's attraction to food is not nearly as strong as its instinctive attachment to the nest, hunger nevertheless governs its activities throughout most of the year. Erecting blinds at suitable feeding areas, either natural or artificial, will result in many picture opportunities.

Eagles, gulls, crows, and ravens (as well as many mammalian species) are attracted to salmon spawning areas to feed on the spent bodies of the dead fish. Similarly, vultures and other carrion feeders gather at livestock carcasses. Many types of fruit trees and shrubs are visited in the appropriate season by songbirds, often in flocks. Robins almost always convene on a freshly watered lawn to hunt dew worms. At regular intervals hummingbirds will visit wildflowers or flowering shrubs which they especially favour. (7) Many birds of prey habitually hunt from prominent perches, specifically those which overlook areas rich in natural prey. In the same way the kingfisher shows decided preferences for snags projecting over shallow pools. (26) When working in the field the alert photographer will find many such opportunities. Situations like these may be made even more successful for photography by the use of bait to gain increased control over the animal's movements.

Humming on Cue

On the west coast the rufous hummingbird shows a particular fondness for the nectar of the flowering red currant bush. One spring I stationed myself near such a shrub, knowing from previous observation that it was regularly visited by hummingbirds. My major problem proved to be the shallow depth of field resulting from the high magnification needed for these tiny birds; focusing on their swift and erratic movements was exceedingly difficult. I therefore installed two commercial hummingbird feeders among the profuse scarlet blossoms of the shrub.

This helped in several ways. The additional food source increased the frequency of bird visits, allowing me to take more pictures in less time, and improving the odds of obtaining a satisfactory image. Also, I knew that most bird activity would centre about the food station and this made focusing easier. By masking the feeding station itself with blooms and foliage (kept fresh by frequent sprays of water), and carefully angling the camera, I was able to take a series of photographs in which the birds appeared to be feeding on flowers when in fact they were at the station. This particular ruse allowed me to prefocus with great precision. Finally, the bush became such an attraction that one male hummer claimed it as his own, perching right in the shrub only a few metres from the camera throughout one full day, driving other visitors away but allowing me to photograph him at leisure. (7)

This is just one example of how the feeding habits of the bird may be exploited. I have used a similar technique to photograph robins feeding in apple trees, hanging several extra apples in a way that improved the chances of photographing them from the position of the blind. In the same way a tray of bird seed may be placed in a weed or grain field which has come to the photographer's attention because of the number of birds that have been observed feeding there. Along spawning streams the photographer may rearrange the spent salmon, building concentrations of them to attract scavengers to predefined photogenic settings.

Cagey Efforts

Live bait, if it can be handled humanely, may prove effective in attracting hungry birds of prey. Ideally suited for such a ploy is the great grey owl, a remarkably tame species when approached in open countryside. A rodent, safe inside a wire cage placed on the ground below the owl's perch, will entice the large bird to attack; this provides a good opportunity for photography, particularly of the bird in flight. Ordinarily, concealment of the photographer is unnecessary. A natural-looking, low-level perch placed near the bait will probably be used by the owl while it attempts to puzzle out its inability to reach the prey, thus producing a different type of shooting situation.

In all such cases it is important to strive for a setting which produces a natural, uncontrived and candid impression, a quality controlled to a great degree by the photographer's treatment of background and foreground picture elements.

Using Blinds in the Field

In most situations, it is usually to the photographer's advantage to use a blind when he is working away from the nest. Although the prime target species may be quite approachable, it is nevertheless wild and will be inclined to shy away from human presence. Furthermore, one never knows what species might have been attracted to the site had the photographer been concealed.

Although a gradual introduction of the blind is not usually necessary away from the nest, it should be erected if possible while the spot is vacated. The longer it remains *in situ*, the greater will be the tendency of local wildlife to accept it as part of their environment. I once noticed a large, rusted oil drum that someone had dumped into a marsh years before. The resident wildlife swam by it without a second look even when I was crouched quietly inside it taking pictures. **(18)**

A blind should be made as small and low as possible without unduly discomforting the occupant or curtailing his movements. It should be camouflaged with local vegetation, especially when wary or insightful species like crows or raptors are the intended subjects. It is also advisable to be escorted to and from the blind by an assistant, particularly at sites that are occupied by wildlife just prior to the arrival of the photographer.

Backyard Bird Photography

Although one of the nature photographer's chief joys is tramping about the wilds, he will miss a great deal of pleasure if he neglects his own backyard. Attracting animals to feeders located about the house is easy and exciting, especially during the winter when natural food stocks are low. Added to the convenience of working at home is the fact that the house itself may be used as a blind. (Fig. 10)

Imagine waking up one cold morning in January. An overnight snowfall has blanketed the outside world in fresh, shimmering whites. Against this pristine backdrop the view from the photographer's window is spectacular. Warily poised on a bird feeder, in brilliant scarlet plumage, is a male cardinal. Two blue jays swoop in from the fence and drive it away. They pound at sunflower seeds, fill their crops and leave amidst raucous calls. Their launch sends a shower of fresh snow against the window. The feeder is quickly filled again by smaller birds—red polls, tree sparrows, gold and purple finches. A hairy woodpecker flutters to the suet log and jackhammers its way into the frozen fuel. The sweet winter song of a chickadee sifts into the photographer's ears through the glass. Suddenly every bird freezes in position. A sharp-shinned hawk flashes past and drives a flock of dark-eyed juncos into the hedge. A ring-necked pheasant tip-toes back into cover and a cottontail lopes hesitantly across the lawn. The birds in the feeder suddenly scatter in all directions and the twitching nose of a red squirrel appears over the edge. The photographer has just finished his first roll of film and takes time out to relax and have another cup of coffee.

A suburbanite can expect to attract at least twenty animal species to his backyard over the course of the winter. An apartment dweller can induce half this many to his balcony and anyone lucky enough to live in a rural setting may get the feeling he is operating a game farm. During the winter, wildlife has two basic requirements—food and shelter. If the effort is made to provide these necessities, photographic possibilities will abound.

The subject of attracting wildlife to the backyard is dealt with only briefly here and the photographer is advised to consult the wealth of publications devoted to this popular topic.

Setting up Feeders
The first step is to place two or three food trays about the edge of the property. They can be mounted on fence posts or suspended from tree limbs.

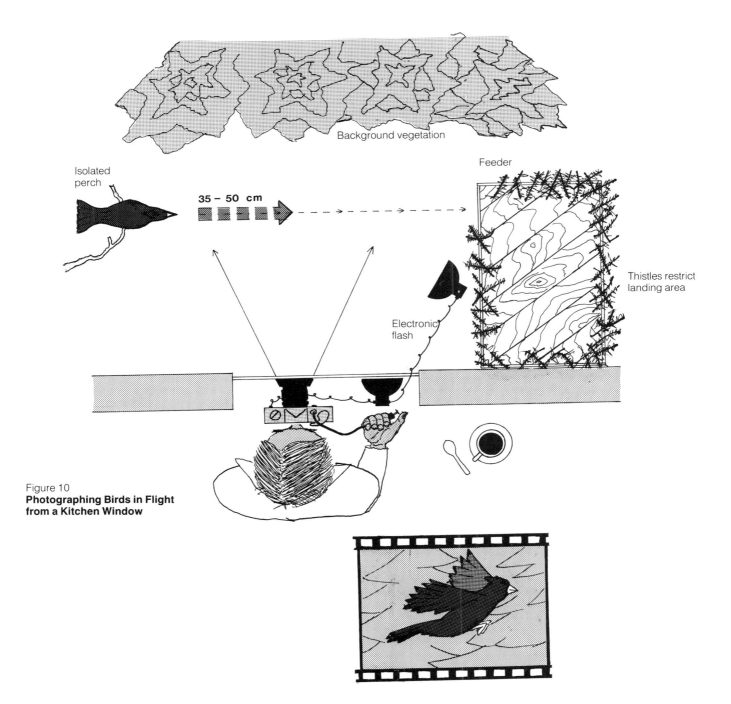

Background vegetation

Isolated perch

35 – 50 cm

Feeder

Thistles restrict landing area

Electronic flash

Figure 10
**Photographing Birds in Flight
from a Kitchen Window**

Once the food is discovered it will be visited regularly throughout the winter and grow steadily in popularity as more animals are attracted by the activity it creates. The feeders need not be elaborate. Simply cut a piece of plywood to a size roughly one-third of a metre by one metre. Nail 19 × 38mm (1 × 2″) lumber around the edge to keep the food from falling off and the feeder is ready for use. In some neighbourhoods, cat-proofing of the feeders may be necessary.

Canapes for Cardinals

Wild bird seed is sold in most supermarkets and is the best bait to use. Practically any type of leftovers also works quite well. Suet is popular with many birds and may be stuffed into holes bored in a log that is hung from a tree or propped up in the middle of a feeder. Birds will probe for the suet just as they do for the beetles and grubs that overwinter in the bark of a tree.

Providing protective cover so that the animals feel safe while feeding will enhance the attraction program. If trees and shrubbery are already present, locate the feeders near them so that quick escape from predators is possible. If the property has little natural cover, a half-dozen discarded Christmas trees can be propped up in the snow around the feeders. **(49)** If the feeders are kept well stocked, a thriving menagerie will begin to develop almost immediately and plans for photography can be put into action.

Shooting Begins

The window selected for photography should be near the feeders, constructed of good quality glass, and generally out of traffic areas of the house. Over the course of two or three days, gradually move one of the feeding stations so that it butts up against the window sill. Rearrange any portable vegetation as necessary. Ground feeders such as pheasants, grouse, quail, rabbits or chipmunks may be photographed from a basement window by situating their food supply accordingly.

Once the animals are feeding at the window, natural perches and backgrounds can be added to the tray. I usually drill a series of holes through the floor of the feeder into which twigs, branches and weeds can be fitted. More holes should be drilled toward the back of the feeder in order to set up a dense background of vegetation. This system permits easy changing or rearrangement of the set from time to time, allowing one to match the animals to their appropriate habitat. Sparrows, for example, usually feed on the seeds of weeds and grasses, while grosbeaks forage in trees, chomping at buds and berries. Evergreen boughs are suitable for most animals because they seek out conifers for protection during periods of high wind or snow.

Another effective method is to drill holes into a limb so that they are not visible from the camera position and stuff them with suet or a suet-seed mixture. Birds and squirrels can thus be photographed as if they were perched on the branch. **(6)** Woodpeckers, nuthatches and brown creepers can be photographed in a similar way except the limb can be oriented vertically to present the birds as if they were feeding on a tree trunk in their normal way.

At this stage it is time to set up the photographic hardware and reap the rewards of past efforts. The window should be completely masked except for a hole large enough for the camera lens and another below for an electronic flash unit that is taped flat to the glass. I place two more flashes outside, about one metre above the feeder. One is used for highlight illumination of the subject and the other to throw an equal amount of light on the background. **(48)** The outdoor flashes are wrapped in plastic sandwich bags to protect them from the weather, and powered by an AC extension cord from the house as their batteries would quickly be exhausted in the cold temperatures. Some of the larger animals may be photographed by natural light but the poor lighting that occurs close to the house and the unbelievably quick movements of the smaller species make the use of electronic flash a necessary compromise.

The rectangular shape of the food tray, if it is mounted so that the short side is against the window, allows one to take frame-filling photographs of a variety of animals using lenses from 100 mm to 200 mm. As the camera must be kept tight to the glass to prevent reflections, close-up accessories are needed to permit focusing within this range. Macro zoom owners will find their lenses ideally designed for this situation. For the first couple of rolls of film, I keep records of the exposure; based on these results, I make final adjustments of the flash placement so that I am able to shoot at an aperture of f8 or f11.

Bird Brains

Soon enough the photographer will find that the animals will ignore the photogenic perches that he has taken such pains to arrange, and persist in feeding behind an obscuring branch or on a lightstand or flash unit with irritating regularity. This situation can be remedied by removing as many of these extraneous landing spots as possible and locating the food more precisely. Some areas may be covered with thistles or other prickly vegetation to discourage birds from landing.

The main drawback to photographing wildlife in this manner is the unnatural character of the setting and lighting. Unless the photographer is willing to build elaborate and expansive sets, framing of the subject should be kept quite tight. **(48)** Nevertheless, the abundance of animals and the ease with which the situation can be controlled lends great potential to such backyard endeavours. A nature photographer with an active imagination truly never need stray from his own home.

Birds in Flight

Making flight pictures of birds is one of nature photography's greatest and most exciting challenges. Flight itself has always stirred man's imagination with its qualities of speed, freedom and grace. Such photography usually entails an element of chance. In most cases the activity recorded happens too quickly to follow visually and the photographer awaits the development of the film with high expectation and an anxiety commensurate with the energy he spent in exposing it.

The first obstacle confronting the photographer is getting close enough to the bird to record its flying behaviour in sufficient detail. Advantage may be taken of the bird's attraction to such sites as the nest, its young, food, hunting perches, courtship and mating arenas, and roosting areas, using a blind or stalking technique as appropriate.

Having approached within range, the photographer must succeed not only in accurately framing a swiftly moving target and focusing with precision, but also in building an effective composition. None of these tasks are generally possible unless the parameters of the flight path as well as the moment of exposure can be predicted with accuracy.

Enter Stage Left

Staging is a technique I use often. Applicable not just to bird flight, it can be used to photograph any kind of fast, unpredictable, wildlife action. A set is designed by selecting such photographic components as camera angle, background, lighting, or focusing distance before the anticipated arrival of the main subject. Birds photographed at the nest or at specially constructed feeders are typical examples of using sets, both natural and artificial.

One of the greatest difficulties in flight photography is focusing on the moving subject and this is one instance in which predetermination is highly desirable. A simple application of this procedure arises when one is photographing fairly approachable birds such as gulls or waterfowl in a city park or zoo. (41) Using a moderate telephoto lens, the photographer sets the focusing ring to the distance that will provide the desired magnification. The subjects are followed through the viewfinder until one flies through the prefocused zone—in effect entering the "set"—whereupon the exposure is made. Accurate anticipation is required to time the arrival in the set of birds flying directly toward the camera. If the photographer pans with a bird moving at right angles to the camera-subject axis, the chances of achieving a sharp image are much improved.

Another example of staging, more complex because both focusing distance and framing are preselected, arises in photographing birds soon after take-off. Ducks on the water present a situation of exciting potential due to the added photogenic quality of the splashing liquid. **(10)** The approach involves framing an area of blank space that one knows the duck will pass through soon after take-off. This is the stage and the photographer simply waits for the duck's arrival. However, the stage must be positioned so that if the photographer pressed the shutter button as soon as the bird explodes from the water, the delay in his reaction will coincide with the duck's appearance within the frame. To do this effectively one must have a knowledge of bird behaviour. Puddle ducks, for instance, take off almost vertically and thus require a different stage position than do diving ducks that take off on a plane close to horizontal.

Curtain Calls in the Backyard

A final example of the use of staging in flight photography can be applied to birds at backyard feeders. In this case the stage is the most elaborate and sophisticated yet discussed, the photographer endeavouring to introduce controls over focusing, timing, lighting, framing, background and the flight path of the bird itself. Close observation of the activity at the feeder and preliminary testing are necessary before consistently satisfactory results are achieved.

The basic strategy is to control the take-off and landing sites of the birds. Once this is accomplished the lights and background may be positioned and the camera framed and focused. By erecting one small, obvious perch roughly a metre from the feeder's edge the photographer will find that most birds land on it briefly before continuing on to the food. The landing site on the feeder may be confined by thistles, evergreen boughs or other prickly vegetation to block off all approaches except the one adjacent to the take-off perch. The more limiting the take-off and landing areas are, the greater will be the chances of success. Keep in mind that most subjects will require a degree of magnification that limits the depth of field severely and that the bird must fly down this narrow corridor of sharpness as regularly as possible. (Fig. 10)

The precise instant when the shutter should be tripped to catch the animal inside the frame poses another difficult problem. Arthur Allen, a nature photographer who pioneered the use of colour film in photographing birds, found that in such a situation, if he released the shutter immediately on seeing the bird take off, he would catch it about half a metre from its former perch. Using the same method, I've found my reflexes to be a little faster (or perhaps birds have become a little slower) and I catch the subject after it has travelled about a third of a metre. By running some tests the photographer can find his own reaction distance. Of course, a cable release is used in this situation and the photographer keeps his eye on the bird, not the viewfinder.

General Suggestions for Flight Photographs

- Don't necessarily try to use a shutter speed that will arrest all movement. Each speed has its special merits. Some of the most provocative flight images result when blurring is used to artistic advantage. **(35)**
- When selecting a shutter speed, keep in mind that the larger the bird the slower will be its body movements, although not necessarily its flight speed.
- Much of the bird's movement can be arrested by panning the camera along its flight path.
- When panning the camera, squeeze off the shots gently, being sure to follow through after each one.
- When good definition is desired, attempt to photograph the bird as it is changing direction. Just before landing the bird is relatively motionless and all the wing and tail feathers are splayed dramatically to break its momentum.
- The easiest time to anticipate a bird's flight path is the instant after take-off, the photographer being able to deduce technical requirements and framing position relative to the standing bird. **(30)**
- Be a careful observer not only of the flight patterns of the various species but also of the location of flight paths to popular roosting spots, nest sites and other areas where birds congregate.
- Keep the camera and lens mounted on a tripod but loosen the controls. This prevents fatigue and allows smoother panning.
- Focusing will be easiest if the photographer situates himself so that the bird flies at right angles to the camera-subject axis.
- When approaching a bird in anticipation of a flight shot, keep in mind that a bird, just like an airplane, prefers to take off into the wind.
- A camera equipped with a motor drive will somewhat increase the chances of success, as well as the amount of film used.

I hope my discussion of bird photography will provide enough ideas to get you started in this exciting enterprise. The information presented here is certainly not exhaustive, but then no presentation could truly make this claim as long as there are imaginative photographers out chasing birds.

CHAPTER THREE

Mammals:
Elusive and Unpredictable

The bear continued to plough through the mounds of rubbish with forceful sweeps of its bludgeon-like paws. Soap boxes, a tricycle, slippery stacks of magazines, milk cartons, tin cans, nylons, empty liquor bottles—all of it was churned, sniffed and tasted by the foraging bear. The prize was finally found—a plastic container once filled with chocolate icing. As the animal's pink tongue began its exploratory caresses, its dark, beady eyes remained fixed on the camera. Ten metres behind me the door of the truck stood open, ready. **(5)**

I looked about at the hills that rimmed the dump. There were black bears everywhere—juveniles, mature males and even mothers with cubs. Usually solitary creatures, they were drawn unnaturally together by the dump's riches. I counted a dozen and it was only the middle of the day. After dark they would really begin feeding in earnest. I checked the bear in the viewfinder. It was still working on the container, seeming to grow more content by the minute.

Up on the hillside over a hundred metres away, there was a sudden bawling and roaring of bears. Hoping for a picture I quickly swung the lens in the direction of the commotion and at the same time an urgent cry of warning came to me from the truck. Turning back I saw that my so recently docile subject was coming straight for me at a run. However, it happened that I was the last thing on the bear's mind and I could have easily run a hand down its broad back as it swept by me; it crashed headlong into the underbrush in a surprising attempt to put as much distance as possible between it and the bears still to be heard fuming in the distance.

For two days I had been photographing bears in the vicinity of the dump and although deferring to their size, speed and power, I had been led to believe by their skittish behaviour that most would prefer to keep a respectful distance from humans if at all possible. Consequently, I had not anticipated my close encounter and the circumstances which precipitated it. However, the unpredictable nature of the incident itself is something one comes to expect when photographing wild mammals.

Reluctant Subjects

Unlike birds which are noisy, colourfully attractive and astir during daylight, most mammals are silent, secretive, nocturnal and coloured to blend with their surroundings. When compared to that of birds and other more primitive creatures, mammal activity is less dependent upon a rigid, instinctively controlled set of behaviour patterns. Such mammalian characteristics present a number of difficulties for the wildlife photographer.

The bird photographer can exploit his subject's unreasoning attraction to the nest. This approach is not nearly as applicable to the practice of mammal photography. For those species that bear their young in fixed denning sites, much of the activity is underground, hidden from view of the lens. Unlike humans, most mammals have a keen sense of smell which can alert them to the approach of a photographer long before he draws within shooting range, or even becomes aware of the animal's presence. Compounding these problems is the simple fact that of all wildlife, mammals are the least numerous.

Despite such difficulties, enthusiastic workers have produced an abundance of exciting, provocative images. Although less attractive in a graphic sense than almost all other life forms, mammals continue to be a favourite photographic subject of the general public.

Mammal Lore

Many of the techniques used for photographing birds apply to mammals as well. Taking advantage of the animal's reproductive patterns and its need for food, using blinds and other methods of concealment, stalking—all these come into play. One of the photographer's greatest assets will be his knowledge of the habits of his subjects. Once I journeyed several thousand kilometres to Yellowstone National Park in Wyoming for the specific purpose of photographing moose. It was early November and snowfall in the high country was quickly closing most of the roads leading to the park's interior. This meant that more animals would be drawn to the easier grazing in the more accessible valleys where snows were lighter and temperatures warmer. However, three days of searching the lower elevations turned up many elk and mule deer but not a single moose. It wasn't until I returned home that I discovered from my reading that, unlike other herbivores in the Yellowstone area, moose migrate upward with the approach of winter to browse on twigs and buds.

There are no reference sources on mammalian natural history applicable to the continent as a whole that I would suggest for the photographer. Rather, he should consult publications that deal with mammals of his particular region. For people living in Canada and the northern United States I can recommend *The Mammals of Canada* by A.W.F. Banfield (Toronto:

University of Toronto Press, 1977) which provides a great deal of information significant to the wildlife photographer. A field guide on mammals should be acquired simply to assist in making accurate identification of the species photographed. One further book will be of value—*A Field Guide to Animal Tracks* by Olaus J. Murie (Cambridge, Mass.: The Riverside Press, 1954). It will help the photographer develop a greater insight into mammal activity in a given area, and such knowledge is prerequisite to planning any successful photographic approach.

Mammalian Senses

Unlike birds, which possess the keen vision one would expect of fast-moving, airborne creatures, mammals vary considerably in the keenness of their vision. Most predators—wolves, lynx and otters for example—have well-developed vision in order to sight and pursue prey. Similarly, deer, squirrels, rabbits, pronghorn and other mammals susceptible to predation have excellent eyesight to spot attackers in time to escape. The slower-moving, less hazardous lifestyle of such animals as bears, porcupines and elephants allows them to survive with considerably poorer vision. In general, mammals are not apt to spot a photographer unless he moves or places his characteristic human silhouette against a plain background such as the sky, or an expanse of snow or grass. Clothing which is camouflaged to break up his silhouette will thus be of obvious advantage when he is stalking.

Almost all mammals have very keen hearing. On most types of terrain, except bare rock, it is difficult for the photographer to approach his quarry without being heard. Windy days provide the best possibilities as sounds made by the stalker are effectively masked by the wind, especially if the approach is made downwind of the subject. When moving within photographic range is not difficult, in game parks, for example, the reverse problem may arise in that the photographer is not able to get the animal's attention in order to gain an alert, attractive pose. In such cases, whistling, clapping or shouting seem not to penetrate the animal's consciousness. Success is more likely if the photographer uses strange sounds rather than loud ones. Rustling small pieces of paper is often effective, especially if it is done in conjunction with body movement such as waving or scratching. Mammals will usually take notice of foot stamping as the sound is accompanied by earth vibrations which they also sense.

Remember the Nose

The acuteness of a mammal's sense of smell is something that humans can little appreciate. Nevertheless, it is a factor of considerable strategic importance in wildlife photography. Scent is usually carried to the animal on the wind. In very still conditions it simply spreads out from the source

The Dynamics
of Bird Flight

40/Lift-off of a Ferruginous Hawk
This photograph has obvious impact. However, such a picture can quickly lose its appeal unless there are other, less apparent, pictorial elements to sustain interest once the initial impression fades. For me considerable tension is generated by the ironic relationship between the hawk's stroking wings and its feet—still planted in the nest. Musing over this apparent contradiction, I notice the hawklet peeking out from behind the mother's tarsus and a touch of comic relief breaks the image's tension. Of course none of these subtleties were contemplated, or even noticed, by me at the moment of exposure.

41/Drake Mallard in Flight

Like the picture of the hawk, this image was attempted many times before success was achieved. In a panning shot at 1/500 second, the exposure caught the bird's wings just as they were changing direction and thus almost motionless. The picture was made at a small city park during a cold winter. The duck pond froze over until more than two hundred birds were crowded into a pool only four or five metres wide—a custom-made stage if there ever was one. As the birds were familiar with humans, I was able to approach quite closely, making pictures as they flew in and out. The surrealistic aspect of the image is due, among other factors, to the unusual evenness of the lighting, caused by the bird's proximity to the brilliant, snow-covered ice surface.

like pancake batter on a griddle, eventually reaching the mammal and causing avoidance or attraction depending on the smell.

The photographer is wise to stay downwind of the subject even if he is in plain sight. A steady crosswind will also cover his scent but there is the possibility of a stray gust carrying his smell to the animal at an inopportune time. (36) On still evenings there are usually steady, convection-caused updraughts which effectively dispose of the human scent and create ideal conditions for photography.

Care must also be taken that no human scent is left on blinds or other equipment erected at baited areas or other sites to which mammals are being attracted. Rubber gloves and overshoes will carry the least scent and should be worn when the photographer is preparing a particularly sensitive site. These should be left outside to weather for a few days or, if time is short, they may be marinated overnight in dried manure or compost.

Mammalian Habits

The photographer must of course co-ordinate his activities with those of his quarry. At the times of day when humans are normally moving about, most mammals are resting in seclusion, perhaps in dense thickets, underground burrows or high in trees. The majority are active at dusk, the subsequent early hours of the evening and again for a few hours before dawn. Practically all familiar species may be classed as nocturnal—cougar, bobcat, wolf, coyote, fox, bear, badger, skunk, weasel, rabbit, hare, porcupine, mouse.

Shots in the Dark

Photographing these species after dark during their most active periods is difficult and not often suited to artistic imagery. It is challenge enough to see the subject let alone focus the camera and frame the scene carefully. Photography by existing light may require exposures exceeding thirty minutes and is rarely even considered. Electronic flash is the most practical source of illumination but due to its limited range it can only be used in carefully staged situations.

The poor viewing conditions of night-time often call for the use of sound-sensitive or photo-electric tripping devices, pressure platforms, trip wires or other types of camera traps designed to activate the shutter automatically. The use of such mechanisms is suitable in some situations, especially those in which the subject is moving steadily along a well-defined pathway, such as a flying squirrel gliding to a tree hole or bats passing through a small opening to a cave. The design and use of these types of apparatus are dealt with in a variety of photographic publications. Most such devices must be custom made to suit the photographer's purposes.

When using this type of sophisticated, automatic equipment, the photographer will find it difficult to exert much personal control over the image-making process, and the number of well-designed, artistic pictures that result will be small in relation to the energy expended. The photographer will gain more satisfaction from concentrating his efforts on those periods of the day (dawn and dusk) when nocturnal species are frequently active and existing light is intense enough to permit a more conventional approach.

There are many species with diurnal habits—ground squirrels, tree squirrels, marmots, chipmunks, mountain goats and sheep, pronghorn and all members of the deer family including elk, deer, moose and caribou. For most of these species activity is greatest early and late in the day, and usually follows a routine schedule which allows the photographer to make efficient use of his time.

Reproduction

The reproductive habits of mammals can often be used to photographic advantage. Hoofed mammals bear their young on the move, seeking out a thicket or coulee for a few minutes of concealment during the actual process of delivery. However, such an event is not predictable as to either time or place and presents little chance for photography. More opportunities arise with these species during the rutting season. The males are particularly noisy and belligerent, being preoccupied with the fierce competition of the mating activities, and are more easily found and approached than at other times of the year. (50) In the autumn, hoofed mammals begin to join together in small herds and become less wary and somewhat more tolerant of humans.

Most other orders of mammals—rodents, carnivores, rabbits and hares, bats and insectivores—bear their young in special sites. It might be a nest of grasses, a burrow, a hollow tree or log, a cave; it might be beneath a windfall or in a rock pile or in a tree nest. Although mammalian reproductive sites are usually poorly lit (if at all in the case of a burrow) and for the most part set in drab, uninspiring surroundings, the photographer can at least be sure of the presence of his subjects as well as some interesting activity—the coming and going of the parents and the romping of the young about the den. (47) If disturbed, many mammals will simply move their families to a new den, leaving the photographer high and dry. Reproductive sites, especially those of carnivores, are not easily found and usually are changed from year to year.

Most pinnipeds (seals, sea lions, walrus) gather on well-established reproductive sites (rookeries) by the hundreds or even thousands to bear the young and mate for the next year's litter. At these times they show little or no fear of man, freeing the worker from many of the concerns usu-

Cold-blooded
Dramas Close-up

42/Garter Snake
Two major difficulties are involved in making a close-up of a snake's head—focusing and framing. To facilitate focusing I used electronic flash, a powerful light source at close range. This permitted the use of an aperture of f22 which provided enough depth of field to compensate for minor focusing errors. Framing was made easier by slowing down the snake's movements. The reptile was cooled off gradually in the refrigerator, a harmless experience similar to what it would go through on a cool evening. The snake was subsequently draped over a tree branch which helped to isolate its head against the background, as well as to keep the animal conveniently elevated for photography. As it warmed up and slowly became more active, I was able to make a series of pictures. Life-size, in-camera magnification was achieved by using a 100-mm macro lens with an extension tube.

43/Trilling Toad

For this picture I had to practically lie down in the same soggy puddle with the toad. Even though the camera leered at it from a distance of only fifteen cm, the animal was undeterred from its mating ritual. Talk about concentration. Most frogs and toads will cease calling when approached during the daytime, but a tape-recording of their song will usually get them started again. This photograph was made with a 50-mm lens and a +3 diopter supplementary close-up lens.

163

ally associated with wildlife photography. **(51)** Most of these species have regular "haul-out" sites for resting and sunning during the non-breeding season, which also present excellent opportunities for photography. In these locations the animals are more easily disturbed and an approach must be made with more caution to avoid startling an individual or even an entire herd back into the ocean.

Habitats

Unlike the bird photographer, who can expect to encounter a variety of bird species by searching an area where a number of different habitats come together, the photographer of mammals must first pick his subject and then seek out its preferred habitat. As mammals are less mobile than birds, they usually seek habitats that provide resources for both reproduction and feeding. A great blue heron on the other hand may establish its nest thirty or forty kilometres from its primary food source. Carnivorous species have the largest home ranges, often covering hundreds of square kilometres. (For example, a wolf requires 128,000 acres, a fisher 48,000 acres, a red fox 1600 acres.) In general, predators work a circuit, which in the case of a cougar might be more than forty kilometres. Such extensive ranging makes them elusive quarry for the photographer.

As the home range of most herbivores is more restricted, they can be located with less difficulty by the photographer. (For example, a chipmunk might need a third of an acre, a cottontail five acres, a white-tailed deer 150 acres.) In most cases he need only find a habitat which offers both the preferred food and shelter and he is likely to find the animal as well. Woodchucks, for instance, eat a great variety of green vegetation, including cultivated fruits and vegetables, grasses, clover and dandelions; they also prefer to dig their burrows in a well-drained spot such as on a hillside or beneath a large boulder or rock pile. Where these two elements come together, one usually finds this member of the marmot family. Deer, being such large mammals, are most abundant in areas of open meadows and pasturage (which provide their food) interspersed with thickets or groves of trees where they can lie up in concealment during the day.

As well as familiarizing himself with a mammal's preferred habitat, the photographer will profit from consulting game wardens, birdwatchers, farmers and naturalists.

Hazards

Although most animals pose no threat to man, situations do arise which require caution. Bears are the most dangerous of North American mammals; precautions to be taken in bear country are well publicized and need no further treatment here except to mention that not a summer passes without several people losing their lives to these predators. **(11)(5)** Members of the deer family, normally quite shy, become aggressive and unpredictable during the rutting season. Bull moose are especially to be regarded with caution, the photographer keeping himself within easy range of a climbable tree. Even the lovable white-tailed deer can become dangerous and in recent years at least two people have been killed by bucks in rut. Small animals, such as raccoons, or even squirrels, can inflict serious injuries if they are molested or kept in stressful situations to be photographed. The wildlife photographer also places himself in greatest jeopardy should he venture afield in camouflaged clothing during the hunting season. At these times he should confine his activities to national parks and other tracts where hunting is prohibited.

Beauty is Furdeep

From a graphic standpoint mammals have little pictorial appeal. For the most part they have rather squat, humdrum shapes which do not lend themselves well to interesting compositions. With the exception of a handful of species their colour is undramatic and lacking in contrast. Nevertheless, they are one of the nature photographer's favourite subjects.

In portraiture, the image is most successful and compelling to people in general if human qualities and characteristics can be attributed to the image. If the animal presents an impression of innocence, guile, demureness, fierceness or inquisitiveness, the viewer relates more easily to the picture. To accomplish this, the eyes and, to a lesser extent, the ears and mouth parts must usually be clearly presented. (19)

Another appealing characteristic of mammals is the inviting lustre and softness of their fur, as well as a variety of other intriguing textures of their body coverings. (36) Consider those of the male lion—mane, nose pad, bridge of nose, back, belly, tail, tail tassle, toe pads, claws, whiskers, tongue, lips, eyes and lashes. The photographer can explore and study these textures with the same artful preoccupation that painters, photographers and sculptors have devoted to a subject like the human nude.

The photography of groups of mammals also provides opportunities for artistic statement, particularly in a graphic context. The possibilities of dividing and designing the spaces within the frame are much greater with two subjects than with one. Each time an animal changes its position, or the photographer his camera angle, a new composition results. Shooting groups or herds of animals, especially when they are milling about, presents many exciting, though fleeting, occasions for obtaining unique images. (51)

Field Stalking

There are few animals that can be stalked by a photographer burdened

Action at the Nest

44/Eared Grebe Threatening
There is considerable displaying of feathers, posturing and vocalizing by birds that nest in colonies. This behaviour helps to define and publicize the space allotted to each nesting pair, minimizing territorial squabbles and conserving the energy of the group as a whole. In such states of reproductive excitement, birds are less wary than normal, and these situations provide many opportunities for exciting pictures. The photographer can record this dynamic action, provided he exercises the necessary patience, taking precautions to ensure that his presence does not disturb the birds.

45/Black Tern with Young
Like the photograph of the grebe, this picture was made from a blind introduced over the period of one full day. Black terns are extremely aggressive to any intruders to their nesting colony. While I was setting up the blind, they repeatedly dived at me, raking their small talons through my hair and forcing me to flinch and duck time after time. Their incessant verbal abuse was no less vehement and I didn't waste any *time getting my job done. Later that day a friend walked me into the blind and upon his departure the colony quickly resettled. Unfortunately most of the pictures (including some fine action shots) were badly under-exposed—a result of setting the wrong ASA speed on the camera's meter. It pays to be thorough, especially in shooting scenes that will not be repeated.*

down with equipment. Moose grazing on lily pads are an exception. If the photographer remains motionless he is not likely to be spotted. Camera position can be changed while the animal's head is under water (frequently as long as two minutes). Provided the photographer does not move while being observed, a similar strategy can be used with other species as well. I have stood motionless and in plain view less than three metres from a muskrat without being detected, my approach being made while the rodent was under water gathering tubers. Using this method other workers have reportedly approached caribou so that the beasts weren't alerted until they received a slap on the rump from the stalker. Of course, in these situations the wind must be in the photographer's favour.

An approach can sometimes be effected by anticipating an animal's course of travel and positioning oneself in ambush, using as much natural cover as possible. If the photographer remains still the animal is unlikely to notice him. (11) In such cases, a motor drive or auto winder is a definite asset as even the small thumb movement involved in cocking the shutter will be spotted and cause alarm. The camera noise is usually of little consequence.

Ho Hum Who Cares

When openly approaching wildlife I normally take a long lens (500 mm) mounted on a tripod. Part of the strategy, especially for approaching large herbivores, also calls for adopting an air of nonchalance. I may whistle softly, talk directly to the animals and spend moments gazing at the horizon as if preoccupied in some other matter. (50) Sometimes I draw closer to the quarry by taking an oblique line of travel, as if my destination were elsewhere. On the other hand a frontal approach shows less movement, only a gradual increase in size of the photographer. In any case, the angle of approach should be chosen according to such factors as the nature of the terrain, the behaviour of the quarry and the direction of the wind.

When stalking, the photographer should remember two important principles. First, keep as low as possible. Because I stalk with a tripod, I have to shove it ahead of me a metre or so and then duckwalk up to it, repeating the process as many times as necessary to draw within range. Keeping oneself folded up near the ground prevents the animal from recognizing the human form. The wearing of a poncho is frequently advantageous as it further disguises the human shape. The second firm rule is to keep all movements slow and deliberate so that no activity is suggestive of the sudden, violent rush of an attacking predator.

Once the photographer is within range, he should settle down, study the pictorial problems at hand and allow ample time for natural events to develop before the camera.

Baiting Strategies

Mammals can be attracted to bait in a variety of ways. Most aspects of this approach are similar to those discussed for birds. Careful consideration should be given to the appearance of the setting, the location of the camera and the precise location of the bait itself. The photographer should keep in mind that the subject will prefer to feed behind something that shields it from the camera unless he takes steps to prevent this by suitably positioning the logs, perches or other props.

In attracting carnivores it is advantageous to drag the meat or fish along obvious trails leading to the baited site in order to broadcast the smell over a wider area. The bait should be fastened down or cut into small pieces to prevent the subject from leaving with the food before the photographer has had time to complete his work.

Peanut Butter Beauty

One of the best baits for most types of mammals is peanut butter. I seldom hike anywhere without a small package or two in my pocket. It has a powerful, enticing odour, a dull, inconspicuous colour, and will stick to almost any type of surface; also, the animal cannot carry it away to eat it in seclusion. I have used it to attract deer, mountain sheep and goats, coyotes, and various species of chipmunks and squirrels (as well as many types of birds). For grazing, hoofed mammals it can be smeared directly on the grass, and for mountain species on the rock ledges and taluses, as well as on shrubs and tree boughs. This gives a measure of control of the subject's pose, the background, camera angle, lighting and other picture elements.

Peanut butter, or any bait for that matter, is best used in conjunction with a natural food source. One summer while hiking in the Canadian Rockies I spent several days photographing the numerous squirrel species that live there—red squirrel, least chipmunk, yellow pine chipmunk, golden-mantled ground squirrel and Columbian ground squirrel—by baiting them to peanut-butter-laced pine cones, wildflowers, grasses and buds. (9) Although these small rodents are easy to approach, they are so active and quick that focusing and framing are difficult. By making a trail of peanut butter dabs I was able to lead them to photogenic sites where I had already prepared the camera for immediate operation.

Splayed Whiskers and Shiny Eyes

Baiting is an excellent method to use in photographing small suburban mammals. It eliminates the time-consuming process of locating their underground passageways or burrows and is also the best way of dealing with those species which do not have fixed dens. Anyone with a backyard

Focus on a Natural Stage

46/Bumblebee on Thistle
Camera angle, lens focal length and focusing distance were all chosen well in advance of the actual appearance of the centre of interest for this picture. To make the most of this scene's colour, the camera was set up for strong, frontal lighting. The framing of the background was adjusted to produce an expanse of pure colour which would accentuate, by contrast, the activity in the middle ground. I also wanted several out-of-focus thistle heads to be arranged informally in the scene to create a lush, bustling atmosphere. Then I focused carefully on the flower which was to hold the centre of interest. Having set the stage, I just had to wait, cable release in hand, for the bees to arrive.

47/At a Ground Squirrel Burrow

This trio of young Columbian ground squirrels is getting its first really close look at a photographer. I caught a glimpse of one of these small rodents diving back into its burrow while I was hiking a mountain trail. Realizing that what goes down must come up, I stretched out on the ground about a metre and a half away, steadied the camera on a couple of rocks and took dead aim on the burrow's opening. After about fifteen minutes, one head appeared and then to my pleasure— another—and another.

can begin to photograph the small mammals to be found there (mice, voles, rabbits, raccoons, skunks and possibly flying squirrels). As most of these species are nocturnal, a method suitable for use after dark is required.

The development of a baited site is the first step. It is best located near any bit of cover—a hedgerow, brush pile or patch of weeds and grasses. Foods such as wild bird seed, bread crumbs and chopped fruit and vegetables should be placed on the ground, preferably atop a flat rock which makes it easier for the photographer to monitor activities at the site. After a couple of days several animals will probably be coming to the spot regularly, leaving seed husks, nibbled vegetables, droppings and other evidence of their visits.

At this point the photographer may begin conditioning the animal to the presence of a light which will be necessary for accurate focusing. A small desk lamp which throws a concentrated beam is ideal. It should be fitted with a red bulb if possible and turned on half an hour before sunset and left on until half an hour after sunrise. The first night the photographer should use a bulb of very low wattage or limit the intensity of the light by blocking out a portion of the lamp in some way. On succeeding nights the intensity may be increased until there is enough light to allow accurate focusing of the camera. This procedure can usually be accomplished in three days without alarming the animals.

The photography itself should be carried out from a blind, using electronic flash light as the source of illumination. In order to make his pictures at animal level, the photographer will need to either make use of an elevated bait site or shoot from a prone position. Many rodents will climb a short way into the bushes to feed on buds, berries or insects. The addition of a small bush or upright branch will not only raise the site to a more convenient working level but also help to simplify compositional problems. It will also cause the subjects to stretch and dangle in interesting fashion while feeding. The lid of a pickle jar can be tacked onto a branch opposite the camera side to hold the food and peanut butter can be dabbed on the bush to lead the animal upward. The electronic flashes may be situated according to the photographer's intentions and he should bear in mind that the subjects will be, by and large, nocturnal. The lamp used for focusing should be placed between the blind and the site, and aimed across the subject for greater contrast and consequently easier focusing. Its light should not be so bright as to affect the exposure.

This approach may be explored at length, not only in terms of species variety but also from an artistic standpoint, encompassing aspects of lighting, subject activity and pose, composition, background and setting. Most work done with small backyard rodents such as mice has so far been of a clinical nature, ignoring the intrinsic beauty and dynamic activities of these creatures.

Photography at Denning Sites

Photography at denning sites can be very rewarding, especially for animals whose living quarters occupy the centre of a rather restricted foraging area, such as marmots, ground squirrels, prairie dogs and badgers. In wilderness areas blinds are often not necessary. However, the photographer should stay downwind of the subject, approach in cautious stages and be prepared to spend a considerable amount of time at the site. **(47)** These procedures will win a measure of the animal's confidence. Food offerings may also gain the subject's co-operation.

With more wary species, especially carnivores, it may be necessary to use a blind in conjunction with bait. All the normal procedures for gradual erection of the blind should be employed. A helper should also be recruited to drop off and pick up the photographer. In the case of a fox or coyote, bait should be placed five or six metres from the den opening when the photographer comes to take his position. Bait placed at the opening itself will often arouse suspicion. A chicken or portion thereof, complete with feathers, is a convenient and effective lure. This procedure helps the animal to develop an association between the food and the arrival and supposed departure of humans. If the photographer is contemplating subsequent sessions, another chunk of food should be dropped when the assistant returns for the pick-up to reinforce this conditioning.

Avoid Controlled Conditions

Many books on nature photography provide information on how to shoot small mammals inside a wire cage or glass terrarium. With this method the photographer first live-traps his subject, stations it inside an appropriately dressed-up container and then proceeds at leisure with the photography.

Unfortunately, such procedures carry with them a number of unsavoury aspects, not the least of which is the quality of the photography itself. Live-trapping an animal is not the harmless, humane procedure it is made out to be. Although not physically injured, a trapped animal may suffer considerable emotional stress, sometimes enough to cause shock and subsequent death. Some animals have such high metabolisms that they starve to death before being discovered by the photographer; a captured female may be kept from feeding her offspring. Then the animal is usually no happier when introduced to the cage set up for photography. Invariably it huddles immobile, with half-closed eyes and drooping whiskers, in a corner or beneath one of the photographer's props. When compared with photographing the dynamism and vivacity of the free-roaming creature, the whole process comes off as a rather sordid and unenjoyable affair.

Fun with Winter Wildlife

48/Squirrel in the Snow
This bright-eyed squirrel has just come up for air while searching for sunflower seeds buried by a fresh snowfall. The hungry rodent was foraging about one-and-a-half metres above the ground in a plywood bird feeder. Evergreen foliage fastened to this platform created a natural-looking background. The squirrel's snow-covered muzzle was illuminated by two electronic flash units whose reflections are visible in the animal's eye. I was concealed in an unheated garage only a metre away, shooting through a partially open window.

49/Strutting Ring-necked Pheasant
Another product of a backyard feeding program, I made this photograph from a concrete blind sunk two metres in the ground—my basement. The low camera angle lent a haughty air to the cock pheasant as it was striding toward some scattered bird seed. A week before this picture was taken, the tree behind the bird was standing in my living room, covered with tinsel and coloured lights. Using a 500-mm mirror lens I focused on a predetermined spot and released the shutter as the animal passed by.

CHAPTER FOUR

Creeping After Cold-blooded Creatures

The tiny frogs were all around me; yet, incredibly, I could not find even one. I turned off the flashlight and moved deeper into the swamp. The night was overcast and inky; I could see nothing. The bottom, partially glazed with left-over winter ice, was hard and slippery in some places, sucking muck in others. Half-submerged deadfalls added to the precarious footing. The atmosphere was saturated with the sound of my quarry— spring peepers. The steady, electronic jingle of their mating chorus was mesmerizing and soon, just as the night had left me blind, the frogs stole my hearing.

Handicapped in this way, I soon stumbled, gasping as murky water was gulped in by my chest waders. One-handed, I quickly struggled upright again, my other arm keeping the camera out of the soup. I switched on the light again to regain my bearings, pausing to give my body a chance to take the icy edge off the water that sloshed inside my boots.

The commotion had momentarily silenced the peepers. The flash-light's yellow beam played weakly over the broken, ragged cattails as my eyes groped for one of the camouflaged amphibians. The peeping started up again some distance away but was quickly drowned by a single song that began to reverberate all around me. I spotted the frog right beside my boot, sitting just above the water on a cattail stem. A small glistening jewel, it was about the size of the end of a finger. As it called, its translucent throat pouch bubbled out, showing a thin network of veins stretched over its surface. Excitedly, I got the camera ready.

The photography of cold-blooded creatures can be approached in different ways. For those who enjoy working in the field, adventures such as the one described above are commonplace. Unlike higher life forms, cold-blooded animals can also be successfully collected and photographed under controlled conditions indoors. Most can be readily approached to within camera range without the need of special techniques.

Much of the activity of cold-blooded animals is governed by the fact that their body temperature is totally dependent on the temperature of their surroundings. A butterfly will open its wings in the morning to catch the sun's early rays. (38) A desert lizard will seek out shade at midday. All cold-blooded animals become less active in cool temperatures. This factor, more than any other, is used by the photographer to control and anticipate their behaviour before the camera.

The warm-blooded animals with which the nature photographer commonly works are only a small fraction of the wildlife that inhabits our planet. Woodchucks are popular nature subjects. If the number that could survive on a ten-acre plot was lined up head to tail, they would probably not exceed thirty metres. However, should we follow a similar tack for the tiny nematode worms that might comfortably live in the same area, the string of life could well circle the globe! There are over a million known animal species and of these more than ninety-eight per cent are cold-blooded. Included are molluscs, crustaceans, spiders, insects, fishes, amphibians and reptiles, to mention only the major classes of animals that can be photographed without the aid of a microscope. In their infinite variety of form, colour, activity and habitat they present a spectacle of unlimited photographic potential.

Reptiles and Amphibians

This group of animals ranges in size from a python as long as a school bus or a crocodile heavier than an automobile to a tree frog that could be covered by a dime. The equipment needed to photograph such creatures is as varied as the subject matter. Magnification greater than life size is rarely called for and simple close-up accessories such as extension tubes or close-up supplementary filters are adequate for shooting most of the smaller representatives. Many species are skittish or dangerous, often making the use of telephoto lenses necessary. The nocturnal habits of many of these animals are compatible with the use of electronic flash.

The tactics for photographing reptiles (snakes, turtles, lizards) and amphibians (frogs, toads, salamanders) are similar. In the field there is generally little necessity for a blind or special stalking techniques. Often the animals may be approached quietly and photographed right where one finds them. (43) With care the photographer can manoeuvre around many subjects without causing them to flee or take cover. Frequently, animals are captured and transported to a nearby area where the lighting, background or other shooting conditions are more to the photographer's liking. (42)

As with other branches of wildlife photography, obtaining successful images of reptiles and amphibians will be greatly enhanced if the photog-

**Mammals in
Their Habitats**

50/Goat in the Clouds
*An inhabitant of rocky crags and jagged
peaks, the mountain goat literally lives
in the clouds. Trying to show the remote
ruggedness of its environment, I
manoeuvred around this billy for almost
half a day, concentrating on obtaining
appropriate background settings.
Altogether I made about 135 pictures,
many of them repetitive. With mist and
cloud seeming to swirl through the legs
of the goat itself, this one comes closest
to capturing the mood and atmosphere
of that experience. The white fur of the
animal accentuated the dramatic
lighting but also made exposure calculation difficult and I opted to take the
meter reading from a medium grey cloud
bank.*

51/Northern Sea Lion Pod

Most sea mammals show little fear of man. For an hour I had been cautiously photographing a few sea lions as they lay basking on a rock shelf on the west coast of Vancouver Island. Then an abrupt, careless movement on my part suddenly spooked the herd. The ensuing avalanche of bodies into the surf suddenly left me quite alone and feeling foolish. This small group returned several times to look me over. Notice how the photograph achieves its balance—by an asymmetrical arrangement of shapes. This keeps the eye bouncing back and forth and up and down, holding it within the frame, creating visual interest.

rapher studies the life histories of the intended subjects. Such knowledge is invaluable in locating the many species that are quite restricted in their habitat requirements. Many types exhibit unique behaviour traits that may serve to guide the photographer's approach. A knowledge of their life habits is a must if collecting for photography in the studio is anticipated. Not only are some species dangerous, but many require special treatment to safeguard their health even if they are held in captivity for only a brief time. A good reference to begin with is *The Audubon Society Field Guide to North American Reptiles and Amphibians* by John Bekler and Wayne King (New York: Alfred A. Knopf Inc., 1979).

Snaps of Snakes

Snakes are distinctive in having no limbs, external ear openings or eyelids. Some species are active during the day; others are nocturnal. They may occupy terrestrial, subterranean, arboreal or aquatic habitats. All are carnivorous, swallowing their prey whole. Mating ordinarily takes place in the fall, followed by hibernation in northern regions. Of the more than one hundred North American species, seventeen are venomous. A bite from one of these will at least be very painful. It may also cause disfigurement, damage to the nervous system, or even death on occasion. A snake photographer cannot afford to be lackadaisical about researching his subjects.

Snakes have unusual and intriguing textures, shapes and colours. Despite their forceful visual appeal, the beauty of the average serpent is not easy to record on film. Achieving a revealing, graphically effective camera angle is a demanding task. Either the photographer crawls on the ground after the snake, or he brings the snake up to his level in some way. Under controlled conditions, an elevated, artificial set may be built. **(42)** In the field, the serpent may be transferred to a branch, log or rock. Of course, snakes can be shot from directly above, and occasionally such views of snake backs yield exciting images.

Another common problem is getting the flexible reptiles to strike a photogenic pose. An uncoiled snake usually means the composition must be based on a single, long, thin shape—a weak element with minimal impact should the photographer wish to include the entire animal within the frame. When at rest, a snake will usually coil up, presenting itself in a way much easier to work into an effective design. In the field, a snake will usually curl up in hiding if the photographer's shirt or hat is thrown over it. This will allow time to station the camera at ground level in readiness for the removal of the covering. The snake will usually remain coiled up for a few minutes before moving off, giving the photographer time to take several pictures. Some species which hunt in trees may be hung on a limb or crotch convenient for photography. Before placing the reptile, the photographer should carefully stage the setting, being sure to incorporate appropriate background and foreground elements and to use the available light to best effect.

Although it is usually preferable to photograph snakes in their natural habitats, working indoors under controlled conditions is sometimes advantageous. Excitable species may be calmed down by cooling them off in the refrigerator. The photographer has ample time to design an attractive set, using natural materials that would occur in the snake's environment. Illumination may come from a nearby window, or from one or more electronic flash units. A white cardboard or aluminum foil reflector is often useful for bouncing light into shadow areas of the scene. Many small subjects may be photographed inside a glass terrarium. If one side of the terrarium is removable, the photographer may set up the camera and make all other preparations, removing the glass just prior to the exposure.

A study of the various snake species will reveal when and where they are likely to be found. A text on herpetology will provide information on how to make captures using snake sticks, how to safely transport and care for specimens and how to protect oneself from snakebite. Snake-collecting should not be undertaken until the photographer is well versed in these aspects, and is prepared to return the reptile unharmed to its original home.

Turtles

Most people think of turtles as slow-moving brutes that should be easy to photograph, yet in the wild they can be quite difficult to approach. With nearly fifty species found in the United States and Canada, turtles are popular, easily recognized creatures. They inhabit aquatic, terrestrial and oceanic environments in both temperate and tropical areas. Like other reptiles they have a uniquely textured body covering, and a body temperature that is dependent upon their environment. **(14)**

All turtles lay eggs. The terrestrial gopher tortoise may only lay two or three, while a large sea turtle such as the hawksbill may produce more than two hundred. Typically, the female scrapes out a hole, deposits the eggs and then covers it over. Depending on the species, incubation varies from less than two months to almost six. On hatching, the small turtles dig their way to the surface, aquatic species setting off toward the water.

Whether aquatic or terrestrial, all turtles enjoy basking in the sun. At an especially popular spot, they may be piled two or three high. Despite their lethargic demeanour, most types remain alert, tolerating little disturbance before they shuffle quickly back into the concealment of the water or vegetation. Sandbars, logs, rocks, floating vegetation, river banks, muskrat lodges and stream shallows are likely basking areas. With care, the photographer can approach and manoeuvre about these sites using a

The Landscape:
A Changing Spectacle

52/Seascape with Gulls

The landscape presents an ever-shifting scene for the camera. To the photographer, light itself is one of the land's most obvious and important moderators, producing effects that vary continually through darkness, dawn, high noon and dusk. Weather and climate also produce dramatic variations—the fiery pageant of autumn, a blanket of snow over a prairie, the eeriness of fog, a storm brooding on the horizon. Water is the land's most dynamic and vital element, in both a biological and a pictorial sense. It tumbles down a mountainside, lies glass-like in a secluded lake or pounds against a rocky coastline.

When setting up for this picture I could not help but wonder at the tremendous weight of the waves as they rolled into the rocks and decided to try to express this relentless power. A low camera angle was chosen to boost the intimidating aspects of the rocks and waves. By their casual indifference to the crash and roar of the surf breaking around them, the gulls became both an apt and ironic comment on the sea's never-ending energy. The photograph was taken at midday at 1/1000 second. I under-exposed the scene by one-and-a-half stops to prevent the details of the frothy wave from becoming washed out, as well as to increase contrast and bring more attention to the gulls.

mobile blind. A permanent blind can be erected near a popular basking spot, the photographer taking his position to await the reemergence and reassembly of the subjects. A telephoto lens of approximately 400 mm will allow the photographer to keep a reasonable distance from these often nervous reptiles.

Many kinds of turtles, especially terrestrial species, may be captured easily and placed in more photogenic nearby surroundings, or even introduced into an indoor, studio-type set-up. The set should be artistically and biologically faithful to the characteristics of the species being photographed. For aquatic species, an atomizer is helpful for keeping the turtle and its surroundings damp and glistening attractively. A polarizing filter will ensure good colour saturation without eliminating the wet, humid aspects of the scene. If electronic flash is being used, the filter's indicator mark should be turned toward the main light source.

A turtle's behaviour may be controlled by having an assistant hold the reptile in place until it calms down, whereupon exposures may be made until the subject decides to move off again. (14) With animals which retract into their shell, it is simply a matter of waiting. Appropriate food offerings may put the turtle in a more co-operative mood, and if natural prey or forage is available it may be incorporated as an interesting, informative addition to the composition.

Lizards Alive

Lizards are quick-moving and surprisingly agile subjects. Most species are carnivorous, and, depending on their size, feed on insects, insect larvae, spiders, earthworms, snails, crustaceans, other lizards and even small birds and mammals. As hunters, many dash about with jerky movements. When approached they scurry into hiding, diving into a rock crevice, a burrow or dense brush. Some species may climb into trees to escape the photographer's lens.

A number of lizard types, especially those with camouflage colouring, may be stalked fairly easily. Others require considerable patience, the photographer setting up the camera near a rock or tree stump that the lizards use for sunning. A telephoto lens of 200 mm or longer, equipped with an extension tube or bellows is best for field shooting. Like other reptiles, lizards may be collected for photography under studio conditions where their darting movements may be more easily restrained. A few species may be caught by hand, but most collectors use a butterfly net—an effective way to deal with the faster-moving species. However, a word of caution about netting the fleet, carnivorous Komodo lizard of Indonesia—some of these brutes are more than three metres long and weigh as much as a large refrigerator.

Frogs and Toads

The life cycle of these popular creatures is well known. Most species deposit their eggs in the water. Upon hatching, the larvae are completely aquatic, having tails and no limbs. This state slowly reverses itself as they undergo metamorphosis, slowly taking on adult characteristics. As a group, frogs and toads possess a number of photogenic aspects. They exhibit a variety of interesting shapes, skin textures and colour. Their carnivorous feeding habits and unique reproductive behaviour are dynamic activities quite suited to pictorial representation.

Photographing toads and frogs in their natural habitat is fun and easy, and yields excellent results. Most species can be approached quite closely, provided the photographer moves straight in on the quarry. **(43)** Lateral movement will tend to cause alarm and subsequent flight. I usually use a moderate (135-mm to 200-mm) telephoto lens in conjunction with an extension tube or bellows. This allows me to keep a comfortable distance from the subject while still obtaining ample magnification. For photography by natural light, a tripod is a necessity. For average to small frog species, I use a close-up apparatus identical to the one I use to photograph insects (explained later in this chapter). Briefly, it consists of a 50-mm or 100-mm bellows-mounted lens. Illumination is provided by one or two small electronic flashes attached to the front of the lens. The flash's short duration allows hand-holding of the camera. As most amphibians are nocturnal, strobe lighting is quite suitable.

For work in a swamp or marsh after dark, auxiliary light is necessary to permit accurate focusing. I simply attach an ordinary flashlight to the lower track of the bellows, angling its light upward so that it intersects the field of view of the lens at the focused distance. Due to the small distances involved, the light beam will usually be wide enough to cover a considerable range of working distances, making infrequent the necessity of adjusting the flashlight's angle. Mounted in this way, the flashlight can still be used in the normal fashion to help the photographer find his way or locate a subject, yet when actually shooting, he has both hands free to operate the various flash and camera controls.

Marshes, logs, streams and river banks are the usual habitats of amphibians. Chest waders are ideal apparel for working in these areas, allowing the photographer to strike out through deep water after a subject and, in shallow areas, permitting him to crouch or sit comfortably in the water while setting up the camera or waiting for action to begin.

In the springtime, wetlands seethe with amphibian activity. Frogs and toads are singing and copulating, and eggs are being laid. A photographer's intrusion into a marsh will usually silence the mating chorus. To catch a frog singing a photographer can usually avoid considerable delay by

Scenic Views:
Unique and Traditional

53/Sunset on Red Deer Lake
Although a sunset photograph often exudes serenity, the image-making process itself is generally one of frantic activity. Light and cloud conditions change rapidly. Often the most dramatic effects last only a few minutes. Camera angles and lens choice need to be decided upon without delay. As the light fades quickly, it is necessary to take frequent meter readings and readjust exposure settings. To make this picture I set up two tripods at different locations well before sundown. As the action began, I became equally entranced with both views, splashing back and forth through the water making exposures as fast as I could of each new design that the sky offered. After about ten minutes the cameras ran out of film and I ran out of breath.

54/Cloud on the Horizon

In this image the dead centre placement of the cloud gives it a weight and presence totally at odds with what we know to be its true substance. Is the cloud ascending or descending? Drifting to the left or to the right? The horizon line, strung right through the middle of the frame, bisecting the image, adds further to the ambiguity of the theme. The scale of the picture is also deceptive. On first inspection the perspective clues normally found in a landscape seem to be lacking. With the discovery of the line of tiny trees, the extreme scale of the image suddenly becomes apparent to the viewer. With a design that borders on the simplistic, this photograph attains a unique quality by disregarding standard practices of landscape composition.

encouraging the amphibian with a recording of its own song. These play-back sound tracks can be made just prior to entering the wetland area.

Toads and frogs can easily be photographed in the studio. Very active subjects can be calmed down by cooling them off in the refrigerator for five or ten minutes, a condition similar to what they are likely to experience on a cold night. An atomizer should be kept handy to keep the animals moist. Naturally, the more care and attention that is given to the lighting and design of the set, the better will be the resulting image. (15)

Many aquatic reptiles and amphibians—turtles, alligators, frogs and toads—habitually lie half submerged, especially when breathing at the surface. Dramatic split-level pictures of this behaviour, showing both the underwater and projecting parts of the body can be made in a studio aquarium. The subject may be herded and contained near one wall of the tank using a clear sheet of glass. Due to the different refractive indices of air and water, focusing on the projecting head will leave the submerged portion of the animal out of focus. A small aperture will provide enough depth of field to render the image sharp throughout.

Salamanders

These colourful amphibians may be photographed in the studio in much the same way as frogs and toads. In constructing a set in preparation for photography, it is advisable to make the stage easily movable. I often assemble my studio habitats on a small cookie sheet. If the animal faces the wrong way, or moves out of the frame, I can bring it back into view or achieve a better shooting angle by simply turning or shifting the cookie sheet rather than trying to move the entire camera and tripod apparatus.

Salamanders are secretive and nocturnal in habit, lying up by day in a rotten log, damp rock crevice or cave, and feeding after dark on worms, insects and other invertebrates. They are not easy to locate. Wet spring weather usually brings many out into the open. Whether the animal is collected for photography elsewhere or shot where it is found, the habitat should be left undisturbed.

Insects and Spiders

With well over a million species of insects and spiders the nature photographer need never be disappointed for lack of subjects. They are everywhere—in the arctic tundra, tropic regions, or backyard, in water, wood or even the bodies of other animals. Many species have a beneficial effect on our lives, pollinating flowers, enriching the soil and producing such consumer items as honey, silk and beeswax. Others help control agricultural pests without the danger of poisoning the environment as often happens with chemical agents. Small, invertebrate animals exist in a dazzling array of shapes, sizes and colours. There are more than 250,000 species of beetles alone. Their life habits are varied and intriguing. With the use of special close-up equipment the photographer brings attention to these life forms which are too minute to be appreciated by normal vision.

As in photographing other wildlife, a knowledge of the habits and characteristics of the subject is extremely advantageous. Much can be learned from careful observation in the field. Reference literature is invaluable in locating and understanding the behaviour of many species. A good introductory book is *The Audubon Society Field Guide to North American Insects and Spiders* by Lorus and Margery Milne (New York: Alfred A. Knopf Inc., 1980).

Equipment Needs

As discussed in the section on close-up photography, special accessories are needed to record animals of this size. A single-lens reflex camera is essential and the 35-mm format, because of its easy handling characteristics, will produce the best results.

The lenses and close-up attachments that are needed will be determined by the amount of magnification desired, the flightiness of the subject and the type of lighting (natural or electronic flash). Most suitable for small, easily approached subjects such as a syrphid fly, ladybird beetle or small spider, is a short-focal-length lens (24 mm to 50 mm) mounted on a bellows in reverse position. (3) A varied range of greater than life-size reproduction would then be possible. Due to the considerable magnification, electronic flash is necessary for photographing live subjects. For larger animals—grasshoppers, bumblebees, caterpillars, praying mantis, garden spiders—a short telephoto lens (100 mm to 135 mm) mounted on a bellows or extension tube is appropriate. (46) Even with slow colour films, these subjects may be photographed under existing light. The use of electronic flash will give the advantage of increased depth of field and action-stopping exposures. Larger flying insects such as butterflies, moths, dragonflies and damselflies are wary of humans, necessitating the use of longer lenses in the 200-mm to 300-mm range, equipped with a bellows or extension tube. (8) Slow, careful stalking, or a motionless ambush technique is required. Excellent results can be obtained by using natural light. Fill-in flash can be suitably applied to these situations as well.

In shooting active subjects, it is essential that the automatic diaphragm operation of the prime lens be retained when close-up accessories are in use. Fortunately, automatic extension tubes are available for most lenses. Bellows must usually incorporate a double cable release system to keep diaphragm automation.

When working with insects or spiders in controlled, studio-like conditions, the photographer can use any close-up apparatus that suits his artis-

Photography in the Fading Light

55/Cranes over Hills
With the setting of the sun it is easy to conclude that further photography must await the next day's dawn. However, one of the most exciting times to work, particularly on studies of the landscape, is just after the sun has disappeared below the horizon. There is still considerable light, reflecting off the clouds and atmospheric particles and softly illuminating the scene. When hazy conditions prevail early and late in the day, intersecting planes in the landscape are transformed into monochromatic layers of rectangles and triangles, as shown in this picture. The cranes in this scene were added after the fact by sandwiching one slide atop the original to develop interest in the large sky region and balance the over-all design.

56/Nightfall on Langford Lake

The exposure for this picture, taken about twenty minutes after the sun had set, lasted about half a minute. Reciprocity failure of the film partly accounts for the coolness of the colour. An important part of the composition is the driftwood in the foreground. It lends depth and scale to the image, and effectively balances the lopsidedness of the horizon elements. Its rough, well-defined texture also accentuates by contrast the dreamlike mood of the image. An exaggerated perspective and great depth of field were achieved by the use of an ultra wide-angle lens (21 mm).

tic purpose. Lighting may originate from an electronic flash, window or skylight. **(4)** White or aluminum foil reflectors can be used to lighten shadow areas.

Outdoors under Natural Light

Successful insect photography outdoors requires that all preparations— setting up the camera, adjusting controls, precise framing and focusing— be completed before dealing with the animal. The photographer sometimes decides upon a subject before he even ventures outdoors, but more often he comes across an appealing insect in the course of a field excursion.

The first step in setting up the photographic apparatus is to achieve the desired magnification. (This is covered fully in the chapter on close-up photography.) Generally, pictures of insects made at magnifications greater than life size must be done with electronic flash or under controllable conditions indoors.

The focusing adjustments on a lens or bellows are not normally used once magnification has been set. Instead the photographer simply moves the entire camera, lens and bellows assembly toward the subject until it comes into focus. With a tripod-mounted camera this is impossible unless he has a focusing rail. Double-track bellows incorporate this accessory, but focusing rails may also be purchased separately for use with extension tubes or single-track bellows.

Next, exposure requirements are determined. I usually base camera settings on a through-the-lens reading of a neutral grey card. Due to the insufficient light intensity outdoors for fine-grained colour film (ASA 100 or less), the choice of shutter speed or aperture is limited. If one is working from a tripod on a calm, bright day, a shutter speed of 1/60 second is adequately fast, allowing the aperture to be set at f8 or smaller, depending on the amount of magnification. When working in a meadow, I often mount the camera on a short, shin-high monopod, a supporting device that carries the weight of the equipment. This requires an increase in shutter speed to at least 1/125 second to ensure that camera shake does not adversely affect image sharpness.

If the wind is moving the vegetation on which the insects are located, I usually wait for better conditions. Sometimes a stout piece of wire such as a section of coat hanger, or even a sturdy twig, can be poked into the ground out of camera view to stabilize a swaying flower, grass stem or shrub. The atmosphere is usually calmest either early or late in the day. Sheltered areas, such as in the lee of a rocky outcrop, large deadfall or growth of dense vegetation will present the fewest technical problems when it is blowing.

Using a Wildflower Stage

Many flowers are pollinated by insects, spiders and even birds. To induce the animals to undertake this vital task these flowers are attractively coloured and shaped, and they supply food in the form of nectar. Because of the large number of creatures they attract, predatory insects, spiders and birds are also drawn to the area. **(39)** Naturally it is a great place for insect photography.

On locating an active flower patch one may pursue several approaches. One of the most enjoyable is to set up a bellows-mounted telephoto lens of around 200 mm on a tripod. The camera apparatus positioned at bloom height will render an intimate, revealing angle on the insect and produce a soft, passive background in harmony with the main subject. **(46)** I usually take a short camp stool or kneel as comfortably as possible on the ground, since even in a bustling location, worthwhile pictures require considerable time.

I try to position the camera so that two or three blooms, or concentrations of blooms, are within the focal range of the camera (an extension tube or bellows limits the working distance of a lens to within a narrow close-up range). Aside from the flowers themselves, my two major concerns are the lighting and the background. While waiting for insects to visit the flowers, I swing the camera back and forth, practising framing and focusing on the blooms that have been targeted for photography. As it is impossible to predict when or where a butterfly, grasshopper, spider, or beetle is going to land, this technique provides considerably more shooting opportunities.

If using a shorter-focal-length lens, I usually mount the camera on a monopod. Focusing distance and magnification being already set, I position the monopod suitably and merely lean in with the camera until the subject appears sharp in the viewfinder.

Flying insects can be induced to visit selected areas by covering nearby flowers with a sheet of clear polyethylene. A concentrated sugar-and-water solution can be sprayed on the blooms intended for photography to increase their attraction.

Special Subjects

The *Lepidoptera* (butterflies and moths) are exotic creatures. They are most quiescent early in the morning while their body temperatures are still reduced. At these times they are easiest to approach and the photographer has time to set up equipment and adjust camera settings. **(38)** Most *Lepidoptera* species have interesting eyes, antennae and mouth parts, not to mention the stunning shape and colour of their wings. **(4)** Consequently, one of the challenges of photographing these specimens is deciding where to focus to make the most of a limited depth of field.

Scenic Shifts of the Horizon

57/Reflections of Sunset
The placing of the horizon line in a landscape picture should be judged in relation to other elements of the scene. Locating it near the middle of the frame can destroy the unity of a picture, dividing the composition into two equal and separate parts. Although this picture's horizon falls in the middle of the frame, the obvious reflections of the sky in the water invite the eye to shift back and forth over the horizon to compare the similarities. Balance and unity result. The algae which disrupts the lower pattern relieves the stark symmetry of the composition and provides the perspective cues that the viewer needs to understand the scene.

58/Prairie Sky

The impressive strength of this sky caused me to situate the horizon abnormally low in the frame. Like the algae in the preceding picture, the sagebrush informs the viewer of the photograph's scale. Its texture also provides necessary contrast to the towering cloud formations. A wide-angle lens (24 mm) was used; the camera was placed close to the brush and tilted upwards to take in more of the sky. This procedure would usually cause obvious distortion of vertical perspective, especially in shooting objects containing parallel lines (trees, buildings). However with a formless, plastic subject like clouds, the effect appears natural yet dramatic.

Unlike the *Lepidoptera*, a spider presents little difficulty in deciding which part is most photogenic. With eight eyes, poisonous fangs and prominent jaws, a head-on view can seldom be matched for impact. Usually where one finds a web in good condition, a spider is not far off. A gentle jostling of the silk structure may bring the eight-legged predator out of hiding. Pictures of a spider feeding may be obtained by dropping a live fly or other small insect into the web. The photographer should make sure all camera preparations are made before the episode is initiated, as a repeated attempt will probably fail to coax the spider into action. The eyesight of most species is quite restricted, the keenest vision belonging to the jumping spiders which can only see about twenty centimetres. As a result most spiders can be approached closely with little difficulty, although care must be taken to prevent shadows from moving across the subject. When attempting photography at the web, the photographer must not disturb the main support strands which are often fine and easy to overlook.

Dragonflies and damselflies are obvious targets for insect photographers. These large, slender insects have evolved as specialized hunters. Four wings move independently to enable fast, exciting flight both forward and backward. Their long legs are designed to hold captured insects which are caught on the wing. Their mobile heads are dwarfed by large compound eyes that quickly sense a clumsy photographer's approach. Stalking must be done slowly, with great care not to disturb the foliage. Many dragonflies have favourite perches where they land momentarily. This presents the best opportunity if the photographer sets up the camera and waits, motionless, for the insect's visit. On overcast days these animals will remain still for long periods of time and although they are more difficult to find, the photography can be carried out with greater confidence and deliberation.

An Insect Instamatic Camera

Photography of small invertebrates in the field under natural light conditions presents a number of difficulties. The low level of illumination means that the photographer cannot use shutter speeds fast enough to stop the action of his subject (a caterpillar on the move will blur at 1/125 second) or freeze even minimal movement of vegetation disturbed by the wind. A tripod, monopod or other camera support is almost always necessary, denying the photographer the freedom of hand-held shooting; this is a considerable disadvantage when adjustments of only a centimetre or less are critical. The low illumination level also requires the use of large apertures, causing a shallow depth of field which is often unsuitable for many subject arrangements. Furthermore, at the most attractive times for photography (early morning, late afternoon and periods of cloud), light intensity is so low as to prevent work altogether if high-resolution colour film is being used.

Fortunately, a simple procedure using electronic flash can eliminate all these problems. It is suitable for photography with a reproduction range of from $1/5$ x life size to two x life size (frogs to horseflies). There is no need to calculate exposure or take light meter readings, as the same aperture and shutter speed are used in all situations. This technique permits hand-holding of the camera, action-stopping exposures and maximum depth of field. In practice the photographer need only focus and shoot. The system works under the same principle as a conventional ring flash, but provides better modelling of the subject at less expense. (3)

Setting up the Apparatus
The key to this technique lies in attaching a small manual electronic flash unit to the front of the lens, or the front lens board of a bellows. As was discussed in the section on close-up photography, extending the lens by either bellows or tubes causes a decrease in the amount of light that is transmitted to the film and a decrease in the focusing distance. With a flash mounted directly on the lens, the amount of light normally lost due to the extension of the lens is counteracted by the increase in light intensity that results from moving the flash closer to the subject. In effect, roughly the same amount of light reaches the film regardless of the magnification, thus allowing the use of a single aperture throughout the reproduction range. The shutter speed, of course, is merely set at the electronic flash synchronization speed (usually 1/60 second).

The flash may be attached to the lens in a number of ways. Adjustable commercial brackets are available and I can recommend one made by Novaflex called the "X-Shoe" bracket. This flash-holder screws onto the lens like a filter. Adjustable brackets can be made at home with the small ball-and-socket heads designed to hold electronic flashes. These inexpensive items are sold by most camera retailers. On occasion I have simply used tape to fasten the flash to the lens, angling the unit so that the light would shine on the subject which, at high magnification, may be only a few centimetres in front of the lens.

The aperture required for a particular combination of flash unit, lens and film speed can be arrived at by making a simple series of test exposures, at different f stops, of an average close-up subject. Alternatively, the test exposures may be done at a constant aperture (f16 or f11 is a good choice) and the light intensity varied by adding successive layers of white tissue paper over the flash's reflector. The photographer will naturally wish to keep notes of his procedures for reference.

Capturing a Wildflower's Essence

59/Bee on Scarlet Mallow
Colour is the key element of this picture. The quiet, pastel hues harmonize with the softness of the shapes and present a unified impression. Black is effective in accentuating any colour and consequently the sharp, solid presence of the bee serves as a reference point for the delicate mood of the picture. The photograph was made from a tripod using a 200-mm lens wide open (aperture f 4) in conjunction with an extension tube to permit close-up focusing.

60/Daisies in the Wind

A good part of the nature photographer's subject matter is alive and moving and there are many opportunities to explore and experiment with motion. Several special techniques were employed to make this picture. The low shooting angle placed the moving daisies against a strongly contrasting background. A polarizing filter was used to darken the sky and a neutral density filter cut the over-all brightness of the scene so that a shutter speed of two seconds could be used (aperture was set at f 22) to produce blurring of the swaying blooms. I placed the camera in the midst of this somewhat small daisy patch and used a wide-angle lens to exaggerate perspective and further enhance the feeling of freedom and expanse.

Field Use

Due to the photographer's being unaccustomed to the magnification of the field of view, one of his early difficulties in using this close-up system is simply locating the subject in the viewfinder. The camera apparatus should be positioned carefully in front of the subject at approximate working distance before an attempt is made to view the image.

With so many accessories hanging off the camera, it is awkward to hold, making it difficult to frame the subject accurately. The use of a monopod will greatly improve the photographer's steadiness without unduly taking away from the freedom of hand-held shooting.

Insects perched on the end of a twig, a flower, or any kind of pinnacle are the easiest to photograph. If the animal is surrounded by foliage, it is difficult to move the camera into range without bumping the vegetation and disturbing the subject. When spotting a potential target, the photographer first sets the magnification. If using a bellows, I simply rack it out for small insects, and close it up for larger ones. With a little practice, accurate estimates come easily. Finally, the flash is angled for the correct distance and the photographer is ready to begin shooting.

Insects Indoors

Photographing insects, spiders and other invertebrate animals indoors follows the same approach as that discussed for reptiles and amphibians. Appropriate vegetation or other natural props should be collected at the time the subject is captured. Cooling the animal in the refrigerator while the photographer prepares the set will make it easier to manage. (4)

Inducing the insect to strike a dynamic pose is sometimes difficult. One way is to set up a branch or twig that the insect will crawl along, angling it upward toward a constant light source. Before introducing the insect or spider, set up the camera on a tripod, focus, and frame, using the very tip of the branch as a reference point. Electronic flashes, reflectors and background props may be positioned to suit the photographer's purpose. The animal will move along the branch toward the light and on reaching the end will usually pose momentarily before heading back down the twig again. Some animals will even rear up on their hind legs, flailing the air with their forelimbs. This procedure will nearly always afford the photographer one shot, and several if he works quickly.

Aquatic Insects

Aquatic insects such as water striders, water boatmen, diving beetles, caddisfly larvae and dragonfly nymphs can be photographed effectively indoors in an aquarium. A small tank suitable for photography can be made from glass microscope slides, or even window glass. The pieces can be easily glued together with silicon adhesive. For small creatures the tank need be no bigger than a box of matches or pack of cigarettes. This size will also help restrict the movement of the subject and keep it within the range of the close-up apparatus.

The container can be stationed against a background made of coloured paper, natural vegetation or some other suitable material. As the background will be out of focus, the choice of colour and over-all pattern is most important. When the lighting is being arranged (electronic flash is best), the background should receive whatever illumination is necessary but usually not as much as the main subject.

To photograph animals which frequent the water's surface, a small aquarium may be filled to overflowing with an eye-dropper. This will eliminate the curve in the water's surface, leaving it distinguishable by only a thin line which will be more in scale with the small size of the subject.

Life-Cycle Studies

An indoor setting is ideal for recording the life cycles of various insects. Like ninety per cent of all insect species, butterflies and moths undergo complete metamorphosis which is characterized by four distinct stages. The eggs are laid, often in a definite pattern on a food plant of the larvae, which are caterpillars. On hatching, the larva feeds voraciously, undergoing several moults as it grows and eventually changing into a pupa or cocoon. In time a winged adult emerges.

The most perfect moth and butterfly specimens can be obtained by rearing the caterpillars indoors. Each species should be kept separately in a large can containing leaves of the type the larva was feeding on at the time it was collected. The containers should be kept clean and fresh leaves added as needed. The caterpillar will pupate on a twig which should then be stored in a humid container—a jar with moist peat moss or soil in the bottom.

When movement and change in the appearance of the pupa indicate the adult is about to emerge, the pupa should be placed in a natural-looking set in preparation for photography. The process of emergence, expansion and hardening of the wings may take an hour or more, giving the photographer ample time to make a series of pictures.

A Palette of Forest Colour

61/Pacific Rain Forest
The average man would be unable to put his arms around the smaller trees (hemlocks) in this picture. The mammoth Douglas firs in this grove tower some thirty storeys into the fog and mist. Acting as a light filter, the forest canopy imparts a cool, greenish cast to the colour scheme, an effect which enhances the lushness of the setting. Such monumental vegetation often prompts the photographer to reach for a wide-angle lens to further extend the expansive dimensions that confront him. However, a short-focal-length lens is just as likely to make everything look smaller, robbing the scene of its grandeur. This photograph was made with a telephoto lens (100 mm) and plays on the remarkable size variation between giant trees and those that are merely big.

62/Red Ash Grove

A simple arrangement of a forest's colours, unusual in their purity, comprises the substance of this photograph. The composition gains unity from the trunks, which visually bridge the blocks of colour, and the leaves, whose shape is repeated throughout the design. The photograph is a simplification, a distillation, of the riot of autumn hues that surrounded me. Made as the sun was setting, the scene is illuminated by light reflecting from overhead clouds.

CHAPTER FIVE

Studies in Still Life

Just as a painter painstakingly arranges a collection of fruit on a dusty table top to be interpreted later in oil and canvas, so the nature photographer approaches the landscape. Although at times he must work feverishly to capture a fleeting shaft of light, rising moon or whirling cloud formation, by and large the land stays put, allowing the photographer to build his designs with care and deliberation. He has the opportunity to size up the subject's graphic potential, surveying its contours and reading its colour and light as he decides on the most expressive camera angle, the appropriate focal length, and the ideal exposure.

Still-life subjects—trees, hillsides, wildflowers, seas, prairies, frost—do not flee the photographer's lens like an eagle or coyote, nor spoil pictures with an ill-timed blink or yawn. Nevertheless, they present great challenges. A painter can design his images freely; with a few strokes of a brush he can raze a spruce forest, realign mountain ranges or spread a field with lilies. No such convenience is afforded the nature photographer. Relying on technique, timing and tenacity, he must work as a counterpuncher, reacting to his environment like a boxer circling a new opponent, alert for an opening that can be creatively exploited.

Land, Sea and Sky: Scenic Photography

Barren deserts, polar icepacks, rainforests, spring meadows, snow-capped mountains, lakes, wild rivers and sweeping oceans—the earth's physical matrix is unimaginable in its variety, and each day is tempered by the passing seasons, shifting winds and weather, and changing moods of light and sky. The landscape has always captured the attention of the artist, and for most nature photographers it is the first choice among subjects.

Despite the land's spectacular qualities, many photographs fall disappointingly short of capturing its real grandeur. Often it is because of overconfidence in the medium itself. When confronting such beauty, surely one just need point the camera's all-seeing eye in the right direction and release the shutter? However, the photographer forgets that only a small part of what he feels is shared by the camera. What he sees, he also hears and smells and touches—the roar of surf and wind, the scream of gulls, the warmth of sun, and the smell of seaweed and saltwater. Moreover, his eyes scan the scene relentlessly, stopping here and there, drinking in its many aspects. The camera is allotted but a single, frozen view that is crammed onto a postage-stamp-sized section of film. It is unable to record the wide range of light and dark, or the subtle colour hues that the eye takes for granted. Due consideration of such limitations is necessary before the photographer chooses the lone segment of the view which will be representative of the entire landscape.

Equipment for a Field Trip

A day of shooting landscapes generally involves a considerable amount of hiking. Such forays are most rewarding and productive if one travels light, carrying a minimum of photographic gear. I normally wear a fishermen's vest which bristles with enough reinforced pockets to hold all necessary equipment safely.

I pack a single camera body with a 50-mm macro lens attached. This is mounted on a lightweight tripod and carried over the shoulder like a rifle. In one pocket is a 20-mm lens, considered an ultra-wide focal length; I prefer it because its treatment of perspective is decisive. Another pocket contains a 200-mm telephoto lens which is usually adequate for isolating specific features of the landscape. The range of these three lenses permits considerable versatility in dealing with perspective, image magnification and working distance. For a photographer wishing to specialize in landscape work, zoom lenses are ideal, saving many steps and considerable energy when precise magnification of the scene is necessary.

In dealing with the landscape, the tripod is especially valuable. It permits the use of small apertures when great depth of field is needed and extended exposure times for expressing the movement of water, wind, stars or other dynamic phenomena. Along with the tripod goes a cable release which I always keep tied about one of the control levers.

The remaining vest pockets are filled with small but important accessories, including four filters of which the most valuable to me is the polarizing filter. I carry two simply to save time switching them from lens to lens. Of the remaining filters, one is a neutral density filter (ND 8X) and the other is an ultra-violet filter (UV). The use of all these filters is discussed in Section One, Chapter Five. Fortunately, my lenses have the same front diameter, eliminating the need to carry sets of different-sized filters.

Other odds and ends include a folded grey card (carried in a shirt pocket) to help determine exposure, and a spare camera battery to ensure that my through-the-lens light meter does not run out of energy. If the day is overcast I take a plastic bag to protect the camera in case of rain or to keep me dry if I kneel on wet ground. I carry half a dozen rolls (thirty-six exposures) of film—two or three more than I normally plan to shoot as unexpected picture opportunities frequently arise.

Landscape Strategies

As in any creative photographic endeavour, the landscape should be appraised with an eye that is sensitively tuned to its potential for graphic expression. Each attempt at a landscape portrait measures the photographer's ability to create an effective visual design. An analysis of the attractive aspects of the scene is the first consideration. In making his evaluation the photographer should keep in mind that the changing character of sunlight is the most powerful influence on any scene.

The appeal of a landscape results from a number of elements acting together, but generally one or two components will dominate. It may be the rich colour of a grove of trees, the drama of the sky, the sweep of perspective, a pattern shown in the rocks or vegetation, or the rush of a mountain waterfall. Once a central theme has been defined, the photographer begins to translate his impression into the language of film. Both his technical skill with the camera and his knowledge of picture composition come into play. He knows, for example, that the colour intensity of the grove of trees can be controlled by lighting and exposure, that camera angle will determine the importance of the sky, that perspective is largely dependent on focal length and camera position, that the effectiveness of a pattern is the result of proper framing and that shutter speed is the critical factor in recording the motion of a waterfall.

With experience, such technical strategies become routine and the photographer develops a systematic approach to making landscape pictures. Generally it follows a pattern similar to that described below, decisions at each step being guided by the central theme of the picture.

1. Choosing Camera Position and Focal Length
Initially the camera should be positioned where it will achieve the most expressive angle on the key elements of the composition. This may have to be modified later as supporting elements are incorporated into the picture. The conventional camera position creates a view of the landscape based on a perspective approach that has a foreground-middleground-background arrangement of picture elements. (25) Almost every cliché scenic photograph on a postcard or calendar is based on this method of organization; that it is used so frequently speaks strongly for its visual effective-

ness. However, the photographer should not allow any formula to prejudice his approach to design. Indeed, countless, stunning scenic pictures have been made which are completely at odds with this convention.

The choice of focal length will be determined by how the photographer wishes to treat perspective and how much of the scene he wishes to include in the picture. These decisions are usually dependent on camera position, just as it is in part based on the focal length of the lens. Consequently, the two steps are carried out simultaneously, usually in a trial-and-error manner which sees the photographer twitching about the landscape, trying on different lenses at each new location, until eventually he hits on a combination which satisfies his artistic concerns.

2. Framing and Focusing

One of the primary difficulties in landscape photography is rendering the whole scene in sharp focus. Depth of field may have to extend from a clump of flowers at the photographer's feet clear to the distant horizon. To accomplish this it is usually necessary to set the lens at its smallest aperture and focus it at the hyperfocal distance (see Section One, Chapter Four). Next, with help from the depth-of-field preview lever, the photographer angles the camera so that it frames only that part of the scene which appears sharp in the viewfinder. (56) At this point the position of the camera may need to be altered slightly to bring important foreground elements into the zone of sharpness. Sometimes merely raising the camera and angling it downward slightly will solve the problem, especially for low subject matter like wildflowers.

Technically, there is little difficulty in making pictures with shallow depth of field, this approach being compatible with the limiting characteristics of slow-speed films and low light levels. The soft impressionistic images that result can be fascinatingly effective provided the motif is consistent and in harmony with the subject matter of the composition. (16)

Framing the scene is usually carried out simultaneously with focusing and setting the depth-of-field zone. The entire picture area requires scrutiny, adjustments being made to portray the centre of interest most effectively. Special attention should be given to the edges of the picture where a distracting branch, or out-of-focus grass stem can easily go unnoticed until after the film is developed. (21)

3. Setting Filtration and Exposure

At this stage it is necessary to consider if filtration of the light is desired. As the filter will affect exposure, it must be attached before light meter readings are made.

Except in those situations where the photographer is concerned primarily with the portrayal of motion, the lens aperture has already been selected in order to control depth of field. Consequently, exposure is set by adjustments to the shutter speed. The first task is establishing what an average exposure of the scene would be using methods discussed in Section One, Chapter Five. The photographer may then choose to depart from these settings depending on his purpose and the characteristics of the scene. Over-exposing will lighten and dilute the colour and reduce definition, giving a lighter feeling to the image. (2) For richer colour, greater contrast and a more serious mood, it is necessary to under-expose from the average reading. (23)

4. Taking the Picture

With a final check of the viewfinder, the shutter is released. If this is not done with a cable release, the camera's self-timer or some other remote trigger, it is likely the image's resolution will suffer. If the photographer is uncertain about any aspect of his rendering of the scene, such as exposure, camera position or focal length, now is the time to take some extra pictures incorporating alternative choices.

Timing and Tenacity

The moment when the photographer chooses to make the exposure is just as critical when he is shooting a hillside as it is when he is working at a nest full of eagles. Lighting, of course, is one of the most important and changeable factors which affect a landscape portrait. There will be a time each day when the angle and colour of sunlight illuminate the scene to best advantage. (53) A serious photographer, sensitive to these conditions, will be on the scene at the appropriate moment, perhaps cutting short a night's sleep or missing supper in the process.

Each new arrangement of clouds, or change in season, will affect the landscape differently. (22)(58) A scene that appears commonplace one day may be magically transformed overnight by a fresh snowfall. The photographer must sometimes wait for weeks or months before all the pictorial aspects coalesce to produce optimum conditions for shooting, returning to the scene to catch the grass twinkling with frost or a lone sugar maple ablaze with colour.

Landscape Perspectives

The appeal of a scenic photograph often rests in its treatment of distance and space, its success in expressing the intriguing immensity of the land. There are problems inherent in trying to show perspective, or the third dimension, on a two-dimensional film surface. Fortunately, the graphic factors which affect perspective are simple and easily controlled by photographic techniques. A familiarity with the following spatial relationships that affect perspective will be of value to a landscape photographer:

- Close objects appear larger than those farther away. Depth can be expressed dramatically by including two (or more) similar-sized elements (daisies for example) in the same composition, but having one larger than the other. The greater the discrepancy in size, the greater will appear the distance between them and the more intense the impression of deep space. A wide-angle lens readily exaggerates such discrepancies; a telephoto lens produces the opposite effect. To be effective, the size, or relative size, of the perspective cues (signals) should be readily grasped. **(54)** Rocks, for example, are usually a poor choice, there being no standard size. Trilliums and caribou, on the other hand, have definite, restricted sizes, readily establishing the scale of a scene. The convergence of parallel lines as they recede into the distance (railroad tracks, the banks of a stream or river) shows the effect of relative-size cues on perspective. Thus, perspective that is dependent on size can be controlled in several ways: by the nature of the size cues themselves, by the location of the camera and by the choice of lens focal length.
- Near objects are commonly found lower in the picture frame than far ones. **(56)** If the aim is to show the far-flung, limitless character of a landscape, a foreground element placed high in the frame may be counter productive; for this reason, some scenic photography specialists (Ansel Adams for example) have shooting platforms mounted on the roof of their vehicles. Camera angle and position are important to this aspect of perspective control.
- Overlapping also expresses perspective. Hills, mountains and trees create a sense of depth when one is partially obscured by the other. Framing the scene to isolate the maximum number of overlapping elements will create the greatest impression of depth. In these situations a telephoto lens will produce an unusual effect, compressing the space that overlapping expands. **(55)(13)**
- Sidelighting effectively brings out the contours and form of the landscape, imparting a three-dimensionality to rocks, trees, rolling hills, valleys and mountainsides. By increasing contrast it enhances the effect of overlapping, placing highlight regions against shadow to differentiate more clearly the receding planes of a scene. Of course the photographer cannot control the lighting in an outdoor setting, except indirectly, by timing the exposure to capture the view when the lighting is most suitable.
- Perspective is also affected by colour intensity and resolution of detail. Atmospheric haze reduces the brilliance and the definition

of distant landforms; this effect becomes more obvious the farther away an object is, due to accumulating haze and other airborne particles.

Water: a Liquid Reflector

Water in some form is usually the landscape's most dynamic component. It has exciting reflective properties in all its forms. The smooth glassy surface of a lake or slough can mirror an image of the surrounding land that is nearly perfect. **(57)** With a breath of wind the water changes character, distorting the reflection to create interesting, changeable abstractions. **(28)** Add more energy and the water assumes an identity of its own, developing patterns of texture and colour that can range from the gold-dappled ripples of a river in fall to a charcoal, gale-lashed sea of spitting whitecaps.

The nature photographer should keep in mind that water readily takes on the character of its surroundings. It is especially expressive of colour, an aspect easily overlooked unless one develops a visual sensitivity to its presence. Like water, snow and ice are neutral colour elements and readily reflect any colour of light that strikes them, although in a more subdued, diffused manner. They have substance of their own, taking on fixed shapes and textures of infinite variety.

Waves and Waterfalls

Water is constantly moving, sometimes so slowly as to be imperceptible, at other times a rushing torrent. Perhaps more than any other subject, it provides opportunity for the photographer to explore and study motion. Surf breaking on a rocky beach, the plunge of water over a cliff or the gentle trickling of a summer stream can be recorded in many unique and interesting ways.

Exposure duration is of special technical significance when one is shooting any moving subject. Slower shutter speeds that allow the water's image to be traced over the film surface produce soft, flowing, sensuous results. **(29)** A setting of 1/60 second will achieve considerable blur in a tight shot of a waterfall, but speeds of 1/8 second or longer are more appropriate for less powerful flows of water. When making blurred-motion pictures of waterfalls and streams, the photographer may want to include within the composition sharply defined objects (rocks, leaves, logs) that will accentuate by contrast the soft flow of the water. As exposure times decrease, the water assumes a sharper, more defined outline. At speeds over 1/250 second almost any water movement will be frozen, capturing the changing forms of drops, splashes and breaking waves. **(52)**

Rain and Snow

The inclusion of precipitation in a landscape photograph imparts a strong mood to the composition. Rain can be warm, soothing and romantic; at other times it may be cold, lashing and sinister. The effect of snow ranges from excitement, celebration and movement to tranquillity and peace. **(19)**

Neither phenomenon is easy to photograph. Lighting and camera angle must be carefully controlled if the effect of the snow or rain is to succeed. An angle which places the precipitation against a dark background (evergreen trees, storm clouds) or a background that is in shadow is ideal. **(12)** Backlighting or sidelighting is needed to illuminate the contours of the snowflakes or raindrops effectively, and it also produces necessary shadows in the background landforms. Under-exposing the scene by one half to one full stop will create more contrast, causing the bright rain or snow to be more easily seen against the darker backdrop.

A shutter speed of $1/8$ to $1/30$ second will give accent to precipitation, the rain registering as glistening streaks and the snow blurring into large, soft puffs. During a snowfall, double-exposure can be put to good use. The first shot will be representative of the entire scene and is made in the usual, deliberate manner. It should be under-exposed by one stop. Once the shutter is recocked (the original frame will stay in place if the rewind button is first depressed) the second exposure is made with the lens focused much closer, on the snowflakes themselves. Magnified in this way, they appear as large, white blobs that overlie the first image, realistically giving the impression of a blizzard.

The Sun

Besides its vital task of illuminating the landscape, the sun is a dynamic subject in its own right. It is best photographed at dawn and just before sunset when its colour and size are shown most dramatically. At these times, the sun's brilliance is subdued by cloud and atmospheric haze, creating lower than usual contrast and permitting other features of the land and sky to be shown effectively in the design. **(53)** On foggy days, the sun's outline will occasionally break through, but at only a fraction of its normal strength, and this allows it to be included in the picture without causing excessive flare or extreme contrast.

The colour and brilliance of the sun give it such a graphic force that it usually dominates a composition even when its size is reduced by using a wide-angle lens. Telephoto lenses give the sun extra size and power and they are frequently used for sunset pictures. However, creativity is stifled if one too habitually associates a specific subject with a certain lens focal length, or any other restrictive technique for that matter. Let the approach to the design evolve from personal impressions of the scene at the time of shooting.

Exposure is tricky when the sun itself is included in the frame. A range of exposures spanning three or four stops may be suitable for the same scene, depending on the photographer's intention. As the contrast range is so great, something is bound to be exposed properly at each setting. In these situations, the most acceptable results occur when the exposure is weighted in favour of the sun itself, allowing its colour to remain strong, while other elements may only register as silhouettes. (25) By scanning the scene through the viewfinder and watching the exposure indications, the photographer can quickly appraise the over-all contrast of the scene. If the needle fluctuates wildly, the photographer knows he must be discriminating in his light meter readings. At sunset or sunrise, I usually measure an area of sky adjacent to the sun, taking care not to allow its direct rays to strike the meter. Bracketing exposures in high-contrast situations is a good idea, and for me it is routine procedure.

The Night Sky

Once the sun has set, weak illumination leaves many features of the landscape in obscurity, but overhead, the night sky is filled with twinkling lights—the moon and stars—which can become the focal points of a landscape design.

The first half-hour after sundown will offer the greatest variety of picture opportunities. The sky remains tinted with colour from sunset, clouds can still be distinguished and the horizon shows a strong silhouette. (56)(55) If the moon has risen, it can be included in the composition without any special precautions. (13) Exposure can be determined through the lens in the normal way, the photographer reading a part of the scene that is of representative brilliance.

With many cameras, the illumination level will be too low to produce a meter reading. However, the light meter can be made more sensitive simply by indexing a higher ASA speed, changing it from ASA 64 to ASA 1000 for example. A quick mental calculation will indicate that the ASA setting has been doubled four times. As the film in use is still the same, the exposure settings given by the reprogrammed light meter must compensate by the same amount. For example, if the aperture setting suggested is f16, it must be opened four stops to f4 to make up for the false indexing of the light meter. Alternatively, the exposure time could be doubled four times.

At exposure times exceeding one second reciprocity failure of the film (discussed on page 57) will occur. Fortunately, when one is recording night scenes there is usually no need to compensate because the resulting under-exposure of the image aptly conveys the after-dark character of the landscape.

To make a detailed, close-up picture of the moon a telephoto lens is needed. When deciding on a particular focal length, keep in mind that the moon seems about twice as large in the viewfinder as it will in the resulting image. As the moon is lit by the sun, exposure is the same for any frontlit subject during the day, (f8 at 1/250 second with ASA 64 film). Bracketing is suggested if the moon has just risen above the horizon, as its brilliance may be considerably diminished by atmospheric particles. **(13)**

Custom-made Moon

By using double-exposure techniques, a poorly situated moon can be moved to another area of the sky to produce a landscape design more to the photographer's liking. The moon is first photographed at the desired magnification. It should be positioned in the frame in the precise location where it is to appear in the final design. Again, cock the shutter (remembering to disengage the film advance) and photograph the main landscape itself. There is no need to hurry the second exposure; the camera can be carried to a new location and the lens replaced with one of a different focal length if desired.

A straightforward photograph of the stars, even when made with a telephoto lens, is disappointing, the stars appearing as only a scattering of insignificant specks on a dark background. However, a time exposure will produce a more dynamic recording of the stars as they move through the night sky. The thin, curving trails of light actually result from the earth's rotation. Various exposure times are effective—from a few minutes to an hour or two depending on the length of the star trails one wishes to record. With a slower film (ASA 64) the aperture can be set at f4, and for exposures exceeding an hour, a stop smaller. A wide-angle lens will record a whirling pattern of light, while a telephoto lens can be directed at a bright constellation, giving more impact to individual tracks.

Wildflowers, Frost, and Fungi: Still-Life Close-ups

Indian paintbrush, elf cap, shaggy mane, shooting star, wild adder's tongue—these are romantic names for small but inspiring structures. For the close-up photographer nature offers a challenging abundance of still-life subjects. Wildflowers, mosses, mushrooms, berries, twigs and leaves comprise the rich, intimate detail of the landscape. As subjects they command the same approach as the prairie sky or a mountain vista; the same design principles apply, and the same technical considerations must be weighed. The photographer brings his skill to these subjects with an open mind and alert eyes, and a strong aversion to repetition and *cliché*. Like the greater landscape, a daisy or rosehip does not fly away at the photographer's approach. They are, so to speak, at the mercy of one's technical and artistic expertise. Although this makes the task seem easy, small, still-life subjects are just as demanding—and rewarding—to shoot as a prowling lynx or stooping falcon.

From potted plants inside the house to a lichen clinging to life on a high-Arctic boulder, subjects are available everywhere for anyone to photograph. This is part of the challenge. To be of value the photographer's image of a trillium or wild rose must stand apart from the thousands of other trillium or rose pictures that have been taken before. (27)(60) Sound composition and technique, and a creative, original approach, will go a long way toward producing images that are well-crafted works of art rather than just a stack of macro snapshots.

Equipment

As for any close-up work, the 35-mm, single-lens reflex is the best choice of camera. A 50-mm lens is suitable for most approaches, rendering a wide range of magnifications up to four × life size when used with a bellows. At reproduction greater than about ½ × life size, depth of field is so limited that perspective is changed little by altering the lens focal length. However, at less magnification the distinctive characteristics of both wide-angle and telephoto lenses become apparent in the image and these lenses become valuable additions to the photographer's close-up tools.

Macro lenses are ideal for making close-ups of still life. Otherwise, a device such as bellows, extension tubes, or close-up supplementary lenses will be needed to enable the standard lens to focus closer than normal.

Steadying the Camera

The camera must be positioned close to the ground for satisfactory coverage of the landscape's many smaller features. Some tripods allow the centre column to be removed, and reinserted upside down so that the camera hangs between the legs. It is also important that the tripod model have extra-wide-spreading legs; otherwise, access to the viewfinder can be inconvenient or in some instances impossible. Beanbags or, in a pinch, rocks or branches can be used as ground-level supports, and once I even pressed two apples and a ham-and-cheese-on-rye into service. Whenever possible, trip the shutter with a cable release or the camera's self-timer. The camera's mirror should be locked up for critical, highly magnified scenes.

When the photographer is working close to the ground, a device called a "right-angle finder" will eliminate the need for him to crook his neck or lie prone on the ground in order to view the scene. It also makes the work much more relaxing and enjoyable, reducing any accidental bumping of

Figure 11
Portable Light Tent and Wind Break

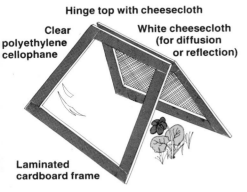

Hinge top with cheesecloth

Clear polyethylene cellophane

White cheesecloth (for diffusion or reflection)

Laminated cardboard frame

Sandwich cheesecloth and polyethylene between two layers of cardboard. Glue and staple.

the tripod which generally will spoil a painstakingly focused, framed and positioned camera set-up.

Fighting the Wind

A breath of wind will cause flowers and other less stable subjects to pitch and sway wildly, making framing, let alone obtaining a sharp image, difficult. The problem is compounded by the common necessity of using slow shutter speeds and small apertures to achieve adequate depth of field. A portable windbreak is useful in minimizing this problem. (Fig. 11) Fortunately, these devices can also double as reflectors to improve the lighting situation at the same time.

One effective procedure, especially at magnifications near or exceeding life size, is to temporarily stabilize the specimen being photographed. I carry a couple of rubber bands around the bellows for use in these situations. A short twig, fifteen to twenty centimetres long, scrounged at the site, is used as a support brace, attached to the camera at one end by rubber bands. I usually leave the other end of the brace free, positioning it for the subject to lean against.

Modifying the Existing Light

Natural light will produce the most consistent results when one is photographing subjects like wildflowers and fungi. Although electronic flash has a number of advantages (brief duration, high intensity), it is difficult to judge how the light will fall on the subject at close range. Ambient light can be controlled much more easily.

As with most types of photography, it is advisable to arrange the lighting so that detail is retained in both the highlight and shadow areas. Film records shadows much darker than a human sees them, even at first glance. Overcast or hazy sky conditions supply the soft, even light ideal for wildflower photography.

In the early morning or late afternoon, the sun's low position may produce dramatic lighting effects. Dust particles and atmospheric haze at these times of day help diffuse the light and soften the shadow areas. White matte or crumpled aluminum foil reflectors may be used in these situations to reflect light into the shadow areas. Such reflectors may also be used to block light from the background, and the shadow created often produces a striking contrast to the main subject, which remains brightly lit.

The direct sunlight of midday is very harsh and produces stark shadows and brilliant highlights that together are beyond the latitude of most films, especially colour slides. It is necessary to soften this type of light by placing a diffusion screen (cheesecloth works well) above the subject. **(27)**

When making close-ups in deeply shaded locations, such as a climax forest, the photographer must be wary of film reciprocity failure at shutter speeds longer than one second. Such lengthy exposure times will be commonplace at high magnifications and small apertures. Compensating for reciprocity failure is covered on page 57.

Whether one chooses to light the subject from the front, back or side will be determined by one's artistic intention. Experimentation with various angles will determine which is best suited to the subject. Translucent petals and leaves work well with backlight. Interesting textures and shapes are brought out with sidelight, and frontlighting will generally produce the greatest colour saturation.

Arrangements on the Forest Floor

When one is preparing to make a still-life photograph, it is possible, but not always advisable, to remove distracting elements. A twig, a badly situated leaf, blades of grass, can all be plucked from the scene. The British call this "gardening," and the process may be used to improve the composition of many pictures. However, if it is carried to extremes, the image acquires the quality of posed, studio sterility and the subjects will look anything but wild. The composition should be controlled, but not domesticated.

Of the many and varied technical methods of shaping photographic composition only a few can be mentioned here. A focal length may be selected to include more or less of the background. The camera angle may be changed so that a pattern of twigs or sweep of blossoms appears more pleasingly arranged. The lighting can be controlled to accentuate important elements by illuminating them more brightly. A vertical or horizontal format may be chosen. The appropriate aperture can produce a depth of field that renders important components sharply, and distracting elements as out-of-focus, less attractive blurs. The photographer can incorporate natural patterns and rhythmic flows of lines and shapes that will lead the viewer's eye through (but not out of) the composition in an organized, directed manner.

Setting up for a still-life close-up requires no small degree of forethought, as well as considerable trial-and-error arrangement of camera, light and subject. When the photographer's imagination works in harmony with these technical considerations, the results are usually more than satisfactory.